What's Wrong With Black People

What Blacks Will Not Say Publicly

W. EDWARD MAKK

authorHOUSE®

AuthorHouse™
1663 Liberty Drive
Bloomington, IN 47403
www.authorhouse.com
Phone: 1-800-839-8640

This is social commentary on issues that affect the black community. It is NOT a
scientific study. These views are meant to stimulate exchanges about the many pressing
issues found in our culture: consumerism, relationships, values, public conduct,
social strata, and matters of mental soundness, and the church etc. We must begin
by defining our community and consider some key issues the community faces.

Published by AuthorHouse   06/18/2013

ISBN: 978-1-4817-5711-9 (sc)
ISBN: 978-1-4817-5709-6 (hc)
ISBN: 978-1-4817-5710-2 (e)

Library of Congress Control Number: 2013909688

WHO WE ARE

BLACKS AND THEIR SOCIAL CASTE/SOCIAL SYSTEM (HIERARCHY)

On April 2, 2013 a survey on a 7 tiered social classes hierarchy in Great Britain was published. In descending order these classes are: (Source: Great British Class Survey)

- a wealthy elite (still associated with the peerage)
- a prosperous salaried middle class consisting of professionals and managers
- a class of technical experts
- a class of new monied (nuveau riche) workers
- an aging traditional working class
- a "precariat" with low levels of capital and access
- a class of service workers

Hierarchy Within The Modern Black Community

Blacks in the USA have their own hierarchy or social classes. Through slavery, Reconstruction, and Jim Crow, Blacks were members of a caste of Untouchables. Advancements were limited within and without the community until the civil rights laws of 60's. Today, not many of those at the top of the black hierarchy, especially church people, would acknowledge a social structure persists. Having studied only the Bible and seeing the world through their particular prism, these "leaders" lack the sociological or historical perspective of a scholar.

Black Social Classes:

- High Ranking Religious class
- Glitterati: entertainers (athletes, thespians, singers/rappers, dancers)
- Assimilated Suburban class
- Aspiring lower middle class (immigrants)
- Cyclical/ Generational underclass
- Ageing Old School (Pensioned)
- Prison Industrial Complex (criminal)

Ranking Church People

The social structure still reflects the lasting influences of the clergy on the community. Jesse Jackson and T.D.Jakes, Creflo Dollar, and the fallen Eddie Long (BISHOP) have great followings and financial empires. Al Sharpton has a news show because MSNBC knows that the Reverend attracts one of the demographics that it is seeking. Intellectuals like Dr. Cornell West and Tavis Smiley do not have news shows in prime time. Smiley and Dr. West have "shows" on perceived liberal media such as NPR and Northern progressive radio like WCPT in Chicago or KTNF in Minneapolis.

Another example of the supremacy given the clergy is Dr. Lorraine Jacques-White, talk show host on WAOK 1380 AM. Mrs. White does not possess a medical degree nor does she possess a doctorate. She explained to a caller that she was in possession of a master's degree from theological seminary in the Atlanta University Center. Consequently, the title is honorific. Doctor is a deferential term used between the clergy explained Dr Lorraine who *loves* everyone. Her delivery is heavily superlative radio: greatest, most excellent, most wonderful. Hyperbole radio tends to diminish the message, for not everything is the best, the most, the highest. In radio promos, we are reminded that she is one of the most influential people in the city.

Highly placed Church people see nothing wrong with self-promotion. Derrick Boazman says that he "would run through hell with gasoline draws (sic) on for his people." Rev. Al Sharpton's promo assures his audiences that he is not going to do anything that is not for his people. These church people love everyone. That is their marketing tool. "After setting the record straight with any caller that misunderstands her, Lorraine gushes: "I love you my brother, my sister."

The church of Martin Luther King Jr. was instrumental in organizing people for marches, sit-ins, boycotts and strikes. In that Al Sharpton, Jesse Jackson, Andrew Young, Rev Lowery, and David Abernathy, Sr. were there during the tumultuous times of the 50's and 60's they carry the legacies of MLK Jr. The church is the strongest institution in the black community. The church was, and continues to be, the place for social change. I moved to Detroit in the tumult of the 60's, during the last part of the Great Migration of the Southern Negro to the North. Since the church was the institution of change, protest, and refuge, it continues to have sway over the opinions and actions of its flock.

Some good reasons remain for the ubiquitous and continuing influence of the church in the community. When something happens involving an injustice, police brutality, or racial insensitivity, the church and its professional spokespersons are there on the scene. Local church folks (family representatives) take on issues for those who cannot afford legal representation. Al Sharpton and Jesse Jackson are the national leaders. Based on their status and the fact that in some cases they serve the community, these powerful leaders are able to collect millions of dollar for their organizations: National Action Movement, Rainbow Coalition, SNCC, NAACP etc.

However, a problem arises with the *prosperity ministers* who preach of wealth as a blessing from God; that God wants them all to be rich. Consequently, those in the middle class, who have had some degree of success, wish to take advantage of the minister's promise for prosperity through following God's plan for them. And God promises them wealth. In short, the church has morphed into a corporation.

The titled minister (doctor, bishop, father) sends an investment and retirement specialist to help with investment. They present seminars which often are nothing more than Ponzi Schemes. I was drawn into a Ponzi scheme sponsored by a group that had meetings at a church in East Point, GA in 1989. People are drawn into a sanctuary by promises of wealth. "Why cannot black people be prosperous?" they ask. The answer is that Blacks need to get together, stick together, and invest. Invest in and support our own businesses. While that position has validity, the truth is that the top of the pyramid prospers in the name of the Lord and in the name of black unity.

The Singing family of Winans in Detroit, Bishop Wiley Jackson, and Eddie Long of Atlanta were caught up in questionable financial ventures. The church leader as infallible icon has been able to hoodwink, lead astray, bamboozle and, finally, sell a bill or goods to the flock, to the faithful, to those waiting for manna from heaven. The black clergyman has his own code words to stir the masses to action: those white folks,

Ku Klux Klan, racist cops, those who do not look like us, those who look like us, immigrants, homosexuals, Jews, Skinheads, enemies of the community, Negroes (pejorative) Black Conservatives, Uncle Toms, sell-outs, Plantation Negroes, etc.

Every presentation of facts will evoke vitriol from those who are very protective of their leaders. I do not have an issue with the church itself; as I want to be respected, I respect others. For some Faith is all they have. But, as I teach, absolute power corrupts absolutely. I am saddened to think that no amount of reading of the history of the Catholic Church and its popes (Borgia, in particular); of the Spanish Inquisition, The Reign of the Tudors (Henry VIII) etc. and the justification of slavery by the early American Protestants will change any views on the excesses of religion. I am reminded that there are theologians and then there are Church People. Church People have no need for theology. Theologians seek to keep church people with the stuff of true faith; with doctrine, with dogma. Theologians may or may not believe in the Bible literally; most see it as metaphor. Church folks see it as the "good book," and as such it is not to be questioned.

The Glitterati

Below the clergy are the Glitterati composed of those who make their living selling images of what black society values. And since society in general, and black society in particular, is shallow and superficial, we have come to accept various standards of what is attractive; what is desirable; and what is to be sought in the American Dream. Lower class blacks do not look at education as a reliable way out. All classes across the spectrum value education; however, poor blacks see it as hard to obtain. Parents start them early playing baseball, football, or basketball in hopes that they might have some talent. After all, glitterati do make more than most professionals with degrees. Some parents do advise their talented children to "have something to fall back on" in case they are not drafted into professional sports. Many do not. Too often I meet their children in Adult Basic Education or jail.

Young people strive to belong to the monied strata, designated here as *glitterati*. Glitterati include athletes, cinema darlings, singer/rappers and the people who live off their largesse: sycophants and hangers-on, entourage groupies who live off the excesses. Unfortunately, the seeds of demise are planted in the nature of the professions. Eventually, the good times end when the money stops flowing in. The percentages vary from 70-80% of those in the glitterati end up with little to show for the years of high income. Ex-NFL players are, at present, suing the NFL because they are bankrupt and/or without medical coverage to take care of mounting bills from brain damage and broken bones. College players even have a worse fate if something happens to end their careers.

Boxing has lost its appeal to whites; however, Hispanics and Blacks still look to boxing as a way out of poverty. Black thespians are limited to certain roles and appear to have a more limited career. Tyler Perry has studios in the Atlanta Area that churn out movies with themes that superficially treat serious issues of the community. He does provide employment for black actors who complain about their treatment or non-treatment in the industry. I am of the Spike Lee school on Tyler Perry: his movies lack serious commentary. In short, his cinema is modern slapstick full of buffoonery and hackneyed caricatures of stereotypes in the community. Ma'Dea' is a relatable character: her language, her mien, her philosophies, her faith. On the other hand, her behavior is schizophrenic, abusive, contradictory, psychotic and neurotic.

Not surprising, black comedians find fertile fodder in laughing at mental disorders. One comedian advised a child to "walk off" the sexual abuse of the "pervert uncle." The Wayans in their in-your-face show *IN LIVING COLOR* had skits on the mentally challenged, homeless, and schizophrenics. Eddie Murphy's movies poke fun at the obese: *Norbit* and *The Nutty Professor*. I must admit that I find his movies to be hilarious, but I can filter what I see. Mental health issues are extremely serious in all communities. People without filters, without knowledge of satire and other literary devices, process differently the images they see on the screen. The young cannot filter what is fiction from non-fiction, cruelty from "just playing." Children should not be exposed to certain types of cinema, television, or social media (internet).

Young people see these professions as ways of making money. Few think about the consequences of career choices. Most jobs of the glitterati have a short duration. Careers in sports last a few years and vary according to the sport. There are few players in their 30's and players in their 40's are very rare. The statistics would indicate that there are a limited number of positions out of millions who aspire to act, sing/rap, dance. Once fortunate enough to become a member of the glitterati, they soon discover that acting is employment. Competing in professional sports is a job. Rapping pays the bills. Singing the same song night after night, week after week, year after year is income for a lifestyle. My empathetic nature tells me that if I had to sing the same song thousands of times that I would need a mind altering substance to do so. How many times could Michael Jackson, Whitney Houston, Marvin Gaye, or Chris Kelly (of Kriss Kross fame) do their hits without cocaine or designer drugs for their preferred high? All of these entertainers died before their times. Did any of them have a college education? Did any of them know of their undiagnosed mental disorders? The status afforded to them as glitterati made them think that they were superhuman. Ironically, there is a certain schaudenfreude (delight at others' failure) about those at the top tumbling from lofty heights. It is possible to google Broke Negroes, Bankrupt Movie Stars, Celebrities having financial problems.

The fact that radio and TV hosts fawn over the likes of misogynist, racist, homophobic rappers gives tacit approval to what they do and say. The NAACP gives its awards to monied people who may or may not live up to the professed standards of the organization. Rappers and entertainers whose "art" is full of questionable language, lyrics, and acts still receive the awards. Is it a *quid pro quo* for donations?

Those with filters can discriminate between what is art and what is not in theater. Unfortunately, those who don't know incorporate and imitate behaviors of the bad boy or bad girl. These histrionics and lingo have become part of the "ghetto persona": head movements, finger popping, and neologisms that come and go: "wassup", "heard dat", "Shawty" (Shorty) and "ya feel me?"(understand?). Youth pass me and don't bother to censor language. Profanity has become acceptable. If I confront them, as I have done in my role as a teacher, they will apologize. Since celebrities do it, they assume it's ok.

Assimilated Suburban Class

As middle class blacks with professional or skilled labor jobs fled the cities and the failing institutions of urban areas, they moved to the suburbs in great numbers. In most suburban areas especially Detroit, Atlanta, and Chicago, the white fled even farther to ex-urbia. In Detroit, the Blacks moved the Southfield as the lower class black moved into Northwest Detroit, the Jews of Southfield moved leaving those neighborhoods re-segregated

In Atlanta, the whites moved farther out into Cobb and now into Cherokee Counties. The Blacks from the city of Atlanta and from the North moved into the middle class neighborhoods of DeKalb displacing whites more familiar with segregation at all levels. ON the other hand, young urban professionals dared to move back into the city thus creating "gentrification" Blacks maintained the upper middle class neighborhoods of Northwest and Southwest Atlanta (Cascade Rd). New homes with $200k+ values were purchased. Those neighborhoods have all the characteristics of their white counterparts: homeowner associations, manicured lawns, active PTAs, aggressive petitioning for city services, strict code enforcement. Homeowner associations serve to preserve the values of the home. They have common interests in their real estate investment and seek to make every homeowner aware of the responsibilities involved. They frown upon tall grass, cars parked on the grass, too many cars on the road or up on blocks, unpainted properties, and pets or undomesticated animals roaming the streets. They put up neighborhood watch signs. The most important: they insist that government does its job.

My experience is with tutoring the children of this social class. I met at their homes. I noticed that they did not lock their homes (low crime areas). I could walk in through their garages, open the door, and enter. The father was resentful of my presence or indifferent. Many were cavalier about paying. Some of them still owe me. They would run up bills and then tell me that they will reschedule. They assumed that I did not really need the money. I do not tutor anymore. We (the males) addressed each other with shallow greetings without making eye contact. The wife was rarely present, but since I had recommendations and spoke 20 languages, and had worked for Sylvan Learning Center, I must be okay. An aside: I don't speak 20 languages and Sylvan's Learning Centers pays teachers between $10-15 an hour. Sylvan's will also send you home, after one hour, if students don't show up—which is often.

Social status comes from being able to afford a tutor. I overheard one of my tutees say to a friend on the phone, "Oh, that's just my tutor." One client would leave me in the house for hours with her daughter. The parent told me that she would "be right back." I was left with the child for 3 hours. The children I tutored did not need tutors. They had learning disabilities or were not motivated to learn. One learns to read my reading. Many were not at the appropriate level for the abstract math that schools are doing now or had dyscalculia (math learning disability). Those taking Spanish were flunking it, hated it, and had no desire to learn hundreds of words or to conjugate hundreds of verbs in 15 tenses.

The black suburban middle class does get it; that education is the most important factor in acquiring and maintaining all the privileges of the middle class.

Their children participate in sports, play a musical instrument, attend charter or private schools' and have learned to manipulate parents with more finesse than those of the lower classes. They address you respectfully as "Sir" and give you presents on holidays. I always had candy; the kids knew I had it and performed for the candy. They also responded to the threat to tell their parents.

The men in these families were aloof and disciplinarians. One father, of lower class origins, threatened to "whoop that ass" if the child was not participating. Throughout the time I spent in their presence, the men remained insular and emotionally contained: Their existence is tenuous. Remaining in the middle classes is difficult. Most families do not have the savings to keep them afloat if any unexpected expense besets them: loss of employment, medical emergencies, major home repairs after a disaster. Women are seen as spendthrifts who waste money on tutors, clothes, and superfluous purchases. Middle class black men would be more Spartan if they had control of the finances.

Knowing that men compartmentalize and communicate with sport trivia and similar metaphor, I started looking at sports events in order to be able to talk to them. These men appear to be asocial and apolitical. While President Obama brought many into the political arena, most do not have opinions on matters outside of their sphere. They do have a strong work ethic and the belief in the American Dream for their children. They tend to be conservative in fiscal and social matters. These are the types of blacks that Republicans would love to attract. The problem with that aim is that Republicans have made too many egregious flubs and faux pas for these status conscious people to fall in line with them.

Africans and Caribbeans may or may not belong to this group. It depends on their level of assimilation and acceptance. First generation children have assimilated into the black youth culture to the chagrin of their parents. Immigrant groups do not trust American Blacks. They confide that they are looked down upon by their American brethren because they are more ambitious and take advantage of educational opportunities

In addressing some of the other classes, I will give representative characteristics.

Aspiring middle class

- Minimum wage jobs (food service, maintenance, domestic service)
- Dependent on social services to make ends meet (food stamps, Medicare, free lunch)
- Income spent rapidly
- No savings
- High School education or less (can't find time, money to go back to school)
- May enroll into GED programs periodically
- Constant unexpected expenses (car, plumbing, accidents)
- Pay day loans in emergencies
- No banking establishment: check cashing and related services
- Children tend to be low achievers in school
- Strong religious faith (high church membership)
- Female headed household
- 2 or more children in the home
- Children are exposed to middle class values which make them aspire to education

Cyclical/Generational underclass and why they remain so

- Persistent unemployment
- Public Assistance (medical/housing)
- Lack of Role Models in family (those who have left poverty)
- Many health and mental health issues
- Generation after generation of dependency
- Large number of children

- Lack of influence of positive males
- Matriarchal Structure (women as breadwinners)
- Education seen as desirable but not practical
- Language consists of a limited number of words used for basic communication
- Food is viewed in terms of quantity as opposed to being nutritious (junk food consumers). Constant eating and over eating
- Entertainment is more important than essentials (big screen televisions)
- Distrust of all professionals
- Cycle of failure
- No access to life changing experiences (travel, books, people)
- Feelings of hopelessness and despair (American Dream dashed)
- No equality of opportunities
- Generations begin at childbearing year intervals 15, grandmothers at 30. great grandmothers at 45

Retired and Pensioned. (55+)

This is a growing class of people who are not employed. They have paid their dues. Many are people of leisure who spend their time in activities related to their retirement: senior citizens' activities, travel, volunteering. They have worked for years in factories or at professional or skilled jobs. Many help their children and grandchildren. It is a growing class of black baby boomers who are relatively comfortable. They face growing problems with health issues and shrinking retirement income. Mental and physical illnesses will be their biggest problems. Since most blacks were hired in public jobs, they do have pensions and/

or social security which appear to be more stable forms of retirement income. It is a social class in that it has definite characteristics that distinguish it from the other classes. It is about 10 percent of the black population but will grow with the retiring of more and more.

Individuals in the Prison Industrial Complex

I call them the *incarceratti*. These individuals provide free labor. They are the Inmate workers who are used to provide labor to city and county governments. They clean government buildings and do public safety repairs on thoroughfares. We see them cutting grass along the highways.

- Criminal Record which limits job opportunities
- Revolving door of incarceration
- Cycle of legal fees that never end
- Constant Probation Violations
- Prison Culture Thinking
- No Rehabilitation
- Substantial number with mental illnesses (bipolar, schizophrenia, poly-substance abuse, etc.)
- Large number of drug offenses (marijuana possession)
- Little support for education in jails (not a priority)

Graying baby boomers, with memories of the 50's and 60's, lament the days when the community was one: the doctor/dentist, lawyer, preacher, teacher, undertaker, and small businessman all lived in the same block. In small Southern towns, the communities had proximity to whites and other blacks of status. Proximity—yes; Mutual acceptance—no. People were given status due to profession (education), skin tone and hair texture, and dwelling amenities. Then, people with electric stoves, central heat and air conditioning, and indoor plumbing were afforded more status.

"High Yellas" and "Redbones" (light skinned blacks) with "good hair" were highly sought by blacks and whites as personal servants or mates. On the other hand, women with "bad, nappy hair" were not considered attractive.

These preferences continue to this day. Those at the top of the hierarchy generally marry those females who do not have strong African/Ethnic features. The wives of professional athletes and other glitterati have white wives or mates who have a certain Latino or Asian look—they are, for the most part, multi-racial in appearance.

In my experience growing up in Tennessee, the larger towns in Middle Tennessee had ties through school rivalries and church services. The Tennessee State Agricultural and Industrial College and Fisk University provided the professionals for Middle Tennessee. My memories of the teachers are not pleasant one. They looked down upon us provincials and laughed behind our backs at our lack of sophistication. I carry with me to this day an aversion to the trappings of the black bourgeoisie or "bourgie Negroes". "Bourgie Negroes" reflected an attitude of superiority and ostentatious excesses: Cadillacs, vacations to the North, clothes from up-scale department stores, landscaped lawns and gardens. They ate expensive cuts of meat: T-bone steaks, baby back ribs, country ham and salmon.

Black Academics, Intellectuals and Pseudo-Intellectuals, and Free thinkers are not part of the structure I outlined, although they might occupy all of these social classes. I have met those in the prison industrial complex who were intellectual in bent. Some people are homeless intellectuals because they refuse to join society. To their minds, those who join society are sell-outs. Other academics are suburban middle class who want to be left alone: part of the assimilated suburban class.

Also, there are those who grew up in the segregated South and never had an opportunity to return to school. These men and women have "mother wit" and knowledge of experience from raising families, and working, and having proximity to enlightenment. This enlightenment could have come in the form of a generous or liberal employer. One senses that they would have been great achievers had they had the opportunity. They are now pensioned and have leisure time to listen to talk radio or dabble in other forms of politics.

Civil rights leaders are eager to emphasize the fact that Blacks have had varying degrees of access to education and employment for only 50 years. While this is true, it does not excuse enforcing caste on our own.

Tribalism

Most sub cultures are tribal—that is: they have their own realities shaped by history, tradition, and experiences. We are all tribal. In the United States the term 'special interest' may be a more accurate description of these influences. Tribalism or our special interest tells us that our immediate group is what matters. We care what the people around us think: family, schoolmates, church members, those with the same political leanings, gang members, goths, sports teammates, corporate leaders, gays, aristocrats, and the destitute.

Those around us do the most harm to us. Most pain and disappointment is of an intra level: intra-tribal, intra—familial, intra—team etc. Friends and family often do the most harm. The reasons for xenophobia are not supported by empirical data. Strangers, immigrants, and they, 'the others', do not have much influence on our lives. The Tribe, la raza, the club, the family influences us the most and does the most damage. I have always been an outsider, so I am accustomed to being non-tribal. I am more comfortable with those who share my views, but I know that I am iconoclastic, reclusive, and dismissive. This view allows me to objectively examine many aspects of group human behavior that appear hard to comprehend.

On Rejection From The Collective

As a black male, I don't necessarily review my alienation from the community to be a singular, unique or personal thing. Once one has been exposed to other cultures: traditions, foods, languages, customs, etc., one can never go home again. You are broadened by the experience and therefore are unable to ever be truly tribal again.

I grew up in the segregated South and thus was surrounded by the values of the time. I suffered from an inferiority complex as a result of constant rejections due to undesirable physical traits.

On Things Tribal

I have simplistically reduced most things to science; most things can be explained in terms of science. As an individual who does not adhere to societal norms and practices-all things tribal, I view human beings as complex primates capable of all that which makes them social and sentient beings. They behave in manners not so different than other animals. For example, there is colony; there is familial nurturing; there is hierarchy; there are ID drives (animal) tempered by Superego [Freudian and unique to humans]. I am of the school that the tribe (colony) affects behavior by awarding or punishing. Alpha—males (metaphorical warriors and gladiators—modern day capitalists) are in control. A chief gives the tribe values and marching orders. The chief is king, czar, autocrat, dictator, despot, tyrant and daddy. Black American culture still retains vestiges of autocracy.

Mental Health

The Diagnostic and Statistical Manual of Disorders (DSM) is published by the American Psychiatric Association. Mental health professional use it as a way to communicate using a common lexicon for labeling mental disorders. Also, the manual offers standard criteria for the classification of individuals with mental illnesses. The DSM comes out periodically; the latest is DSM IV. I became aware of the manual while studying for a master's degree in psychological services at Atlanta University. As I read the many classifications, I came to the conclusion that the guide should be made mandatory reading for all in the helping professions. In addition, anyone with children should have access to the information.

Reading the manual produced many epiphanies for me concerning behaviors I had observed in acquaintances and family. I was able to look at "difficult" people from my past and in my present and see how they were dealing with many undiagnosed disorders. Of course, there is a problem with unqualified people making diagnoses; therefore, my treatment of the issue here is educational. In short, I wish to raise the level of awareness of the many psychological issues we are faced with. There are people and cultures that reject the social sciences. I have been told many times that the social sciences are "bullshit", "crap", "all theory". Unfortunately, those in power appear to share that opinion and look askance at these sciences.

Our correctional facilities are punitive—not institutions of rehabilitation. In the theocracies of the world, those exhibiting mental illness are deemed possessed by evil spirits. Many are institutionalized or incarcerated. Under Sharia law, a kleptomaniac might have extremities removed. Also, a wife showing signs of being abused by her husband (physical abuse disorder), might be returned to her father's house in a taxi. The husband might be suffering from Personality Disorders or Sado-masochism disorder—pleasure (sexual or non sexual) derived from inflicting pain. Even in advanced societies of Western Europe and the Americans, we see the institutionalization of those with treatable disorders.

A mental disorder or illness is defined as *a psychological pattern or anomaly that causes distress or disability*. The list of disorders is long. Below you will find a list of some of the most common, those that the reader might recognize. Then, I will share experiences private, public, and anecdotal. Many of the terms and labels are bantered about daily in jokes throughout the media, and especially by comedians who find it fodder for their routines.

On the other hand, in the educational system, a parent with a child being serviced by the school psychologist or social worker may hear of a disorder but the reference conveys little meaning. A concerted effort to educate citizens in questions of psychological natures is practically non-existent: "Psychology is bullshit; beat that child's ass." "You don't understand some children need their asses whooped." "In my day, you could beat your children. Now you can't . . . that's why we have all the problems we have." Schools avoid labeling *problem children* because the school with then have to pay for the battery of psychological tests to confirm a diagnosis of one of the disorders listed below. The schools only test for a few targeted disorders after school staff observations. Peruse the list; research a mental disorder below. However, **DO NOT**

DIAGNOSE AND ACT UPON THAT DIAGNOSIS. That should be left to mental health professionals and preferably those with expertise in any given disorder.

- Acute Stress Disorder
- Agoraphobia
- Alcohol Abuse
- Alzheimer's
- Anorexia Nervosa
- Anxiety Disorder
- Attention Deficit Hyperactivity Disorder
- Autism Spectrum
- Bipolar Disorder
- Borderline Personalities Disorder
- Bulimia Nervosa
- Circadian Rhythm Sleep Disorder
- Cannabis Dependence
- Cocaine Dependence
- Communication Disorder
- Conduct Disorder
- Dependent Personality Disorder
- Dementia
- Depressive Disorder
- Dyslexia
- Grandiose Delusions
- Impulse Control Disorder
- Kleptomania
- Mathematics Disorder (Dyscalculia)

- Narcissistic personality
- Obsessive-compulsive Disorder /Personality(OCDP)
- Oppositional Defiant Disorder (ODD)
- Pain Disorder
- Paranoid Personality Disorder
- Personality Disorder
- Phobic Disorder
- Physical Abuse
- Poly—substance-related Disorder
- Post Traumatic Stress Disorder
- Pyromania
- Reading Disorder
- Sado—Masochism
- Seasonal Affective Disorder
- Schizophrenia

American Negroes, Blacks, African-American, and all the other members of the Diaspora (Africa to the Caribbean to Latin American) suffer and have suffered many of these mental illnesses. They have lived with significant others who have suffered from these disorders. Our young people are being destroyed by the consequences and ramifications of undiagnosed psychological problems. If you are in a home with mental disorders, you need to look at what is producing the behaviors. There is always a reason or cause. The schools may or may not help. This is a period of draconian cuts in school budgets. Mental health is not a priority

Using the manual, I have self-diagnosed myself with ADHD and Obsessive—Compulsive Disorder based in the dysfunctional nature of my childhood and/or body chemistry. I am unable to concentrate for long periods of time, thus it is hard for me to complete tasks. I started piano lessons and lost interest. I have attempted to author more than 12 books. This is the first to be completed. My handwriting is characteristically that of a person with ADHD: great variety of lettering with caps and small letters used inconsistently, impulsive/interrupting behavior. In classes, I never raised my hand; I just blurted things out. In addition, I am inattentive and hyperactive. I cannot be still for a long period of time. Many people consider me rude or arrogant because I pass notes during meetings and avoid social situations. I am impatient because a few minutes can seem like an hour. Most drivers on the road get in my way, and I am dismissive of people who are more deliberate in their movements. It is my desire that you observe noticeable traits in those around you. Look for the following:

- Easily distracted: missing details, forgetting things, quickly changing from one activity to another
- Problems maintaining focus on the task at hand
- Demonstrating boredom with task at hand unless enjoyable
- Daydreaming
- Processing of information in different manners: generally slower., appearing confused
- Struggling to follow instructions
- Fidgeting and squirming
- Non-stop talking
- Problems organizing
- Displaying a disheveled appearance

I would like the population at large to understand more about the experience of those coping with disorders. While good things can come from obsessive-compulsives who devote much energy and attention to useful activities, their lives would be made easier if others understood that obsessive-compulsives do not receive pleasure from their repetitive practices. I do not have many ritual types of behaviors such as excessive hand washing; however, I do check the iron and stove often. I obsess over matters of my personal financial and physical security. I compulsively pick up the litter in the block alongside my house. I am able to function but some individuals need treatment if their practices interfere with daily functioning.

Black people experience all the mental disorders found in the DSM. However, some of these disorders are more prevalent and destructive. The Eating Disorders such as Anorexia Nervosa and Bulimia used to be considered white girl diseases related to a distorted view/perception of the body. Now, a growing percent of black youths are overweight or obese. Types of eating disorders are threatening the community with diet related diseases such as diabetes, heart disease, and cancer. Personally, I have not seen some children when they were not eating.

This includes children in my family. Lower class Blacks want their children to eat. The quantity is more important than the quality. The diet of the poor kid is replete with chips, cookies, fat laden meat, and corn syrup products—addictively sweet. The middle class kid gets more balanced meals but still has access to junk food. Consequently, there is an epidemic of overweight minority children. A recent study showed the problem to be that most parents do not see their children as obese. On the other hand, they do see small children as underfed. Adults who lose weight, Al Sharpton comes to mind, are seen as not well if they get too small. I have been often told to get some meat on my bones at 5'7" 155lbs, 32" waist—my consistent size.

The substance abuse disorders are causing the most direct devastation in the black community: alcohol, tobacco, cannabis, cocaine, crack, heroin, and the multiple uses: (poly-related substances disorders. Those with multiple disorders such as ADHD, Personality Disorders, and Learning Disabilities are more apt to abuse substances. People without access to mental health help, self medicate with mind altering chemicals. Alcohol and tobacco are legal so they are readily availability.

Cannabis, in the form of the blunt (marijuana stuffed into cigar papers after dumping the tobacco) is now common among even the very young. Those incarcerated I have encountered confess to having begun smoking as early as 8 or 9 years old. As a result, their emotional, mental, and psychological growth stopped at that age. As a result, they are unable to make good decisions. Their heads have been in a smoke induced haze for half their lives.

When I started picking up litter, I was amazed at the number of discarded cigar tobacco and their plastic containers. I lamented that the kids were smoking cigars: Blounts, White Owl, etc. A young man in my class at a correctional institution educated me to the fact that they were smoking "blunts." He confided that he got high every day before high school—after all, that's why they call it high school. Peer pressure remains very powerful. I think that the use of cannabis is much higher than the statistics would indicate. In fact, a client in a rehab center told me that he stole his mother's stash and smoked all the time. Others smoked with their parents. A middle school student shared that his father was too high to help him with homework. Other parents are selling drugs from the house.

In some neighborhoods, there are several places where you can go for various drugs. Marijuana has lost its taboo and is more or less accepted as an extra money hustle. Some teens sell drugs from their parents' home when the parents are gone. Others take and fill orders and make deliveries. Since I came from a home where all substances legal and illegal were prohibited, it took a long time to accept that all types of substances are available from alcohol to designer drugs. Parents should be aware of what they should look for:

- Behavioral Changes: sleeping pattern, withdrawal, mood swings.
- Changes in Acquaintances
- Acrid smell of marijuana
- A need for money leading to theft
- Munching as a result of greater appetites
- Many trips in and out'
- Mouthwash and fragrances to hide smells
- Disinterest in normal activities
- Loss of motivation

Members of the black Glitterati: athletes, singers, actors, rappers have the seeds of their demise sewn into the exigencies of their professions. Most of them succumb to polysubstance abuse. Michael Jackson's hair mishap with fire made him dependent on pain pills. His sleep disorders made him more and more dependent on sleep inducing drugs. MJ ended up taking cocktails of drugs to make it through performances.

Harry Edwards is the expert here on the black American athletes. In addition, over 70% are poor and uninsurable after retirement as they suffer from injuries sustained in their careers. The cable series *Unsung* and *Lifeafter* detail the tragic life of the black glitterati and Tina Marie. Singer after singer, actor after actor, indulged in heaving drinking, pills, hallucinogens, cocaine, and designer drug use. All of which caused their deaths or their fall from grace: Diana Ross, David Ruffian, James Brown, Jimi Hendricks, Chris Kelly, DMX, Tupac. Ironically, for the poor, this is the way out: professional sports, rapping/singing, acting. The community holds these icons up as models of success. I do not see an increasing emphasis on academics and scholarship being promoted as a way up and out in a large segment of the black community. Poor people seek quick money from physical attributes, which fade. Middle class and the upper classes seek lasting security with education, contacts, and the amassing of material wealth and influence.

There is a **Dependence Disorder** that results from heavy drug use. Heavy "blunt" smokers are not achievers. Some researchers are convinced that excessive use of certain mind altering drugs such as cannabis is directly linked to loss of the drive to achieve. Drug use creates sons and daughters who will never be able to support themselves. They are overwhelmed by the world of responsibility. Some siblings leave the nest; go to college; enlist into military service; or seek independence from their parents in various ways. The Dependent Types know they will never be able to support themselves: the ones who the parents tolerate and make excuses for. They think the world is unfair; that the world owes them a living and their parents and siblings should support them until they can *get on their feet*. The community has thousands of unemployed dependents who cannot pass a drug test; who cannot hold a job; who will not dress or conform to workplace standards. It is a problem that needs to be addressed. The black family has generally taken care of all dependents because they are viewed as being different and in need of a little more time to *get it together*. Family is family. Black neighborhoods know the types. They get up late, walk the streets smoking and drinking. They have given up on looking for a job. Eventually, they may or may not be put out of the house. The threat is always there.

Physical Abuse is listed in the DSM. It details how people react to being physically abused. This is an almost taboo subject in the unenlightened black community. By unenlightened I mean those who have taken an avoidance, non-approach of looking the other way, or explaining away, or defending, or misplacing blame in matters of physical (including sexual), and egregious psychological abuse. In my interviews with incarcerated males and females, I have concluded that incestuous and step-sexual relationships occur in significant numbers. In fact, some criminal behavior might have roots in such abuse. Males and females are victims. Glitterati such as Oprah Winfrey, Tyler Perry, and Sugar Ray Leonard have been sexually molested by family or authoritarian figures. 1 in 4 females and 1 in 6 males will be sexually preyed upon by family or individuals with access: momma's boyfriend, neighbors, babysitter, internet predators.

A child who speaks up has to be very careful. Such charges can destroy the already weak family structure. Then the victimized child will have the added burden of having been the instrument of that destruction. If the parent is in a dependent position to the abuser, she (usually it is a woman) might be sacrificing all types of securities to confront the predator. Others parents will be in denial or paralyzed by the information. When inmates shared that unsolicited information with me, I used to see it as a ploy to get sympathy, because I was never molested by adults as a child. I have learned the sad truth of their stories.

My interviews (my next book) with the incarcerated suggest that there is more molestation that is unreported. Uncles, cousins, neighbors, siblings' friends, and authority figures tend to be the offenders. Males are the culprits most but not all the time. Males are less likely to expose abuse on any level. I asked one inmate why he did not tell his mother. He said that he heard his mother say, after viewing a case of sexual molestation, that she would kill anyone who messed with her kids, that she would shoot them dead and go to jail. He said that he did not want his mother to kill her brother. Another young man did tell his mother about his father molesting him, years after his father died, but she never spoke of it. Taboo! Taboo! Too Taboo!

Females, unfortunately, are objectified in our society and, as a result, they are seen as such. Many men in black communities do not respect the laws on making sexual contact. If they did, we would not have so many pregnant girls under the age of 16 (age of consent in Georgia). The impregnator is rarely prosecuted for statutory rape. The community saying is: "Babies having babies." Since many women started having children in their mid teens they do not have much to say on the subject. The state will support them. And the fathers (dependent types) will provide labor for the prison industrial complex. These men will be in and out of jail for petty crimes and failure to pay child support.

Non-sexual abuse also destroys lives. An overwhelming majority of black parents believe in "whooping ass." When I bring up the topic, my clients, inmates, or students share how they were disciplined as children. They do not consider what they do as abusive: slapping, punching, nude belt or strop beating. This form of discipline is so strongly ingrained in the community that they react emotionally to suggested alternatives. I tell them that if they have to discipline their children daily with beating, there must be other psychological issues. You need to look at the cause. In psychology the term for the immediate cessation of an unwanted behavior is called "extinction." You tell a child to stop doing what they are doing, and they STOP it—immediately. Stop hitting your brother/ sister. Stop pilfering little things. Stop acting up in school. Just stop it. If they stop and never do it again, there is an extinction of the behavior. Extinction is extremely rare.

Parents still think that they can and should beat the devil and demons out of their children. They also beat their pets for doing things that pets do. Physical punishment teaches that violence is a legitimate way to solve problems. In many cases, it is abuse driven by generationally approved ways to control mercurial, rebellious children. Some say it is a continuation of plantation discipline: "Beat em like slaves." I have had classroom discussions about the many different types of abusive discipline practiced.

1. *Go get your own switch for a beat down* (severe beating).—This is masochistic in itself in that the child never returns with an instrument of punishment that is big enough.
2. *Fling anything available*: shoe (most popular with old school women), iron, broom, pots and pans, light furniture, etc.
3. *Knock them down:* face, head, or chest (male discipline).
4. *Surprise attack*: wait until the child is asleep or in the bathroom— naked is best.
5. *All types of psychological abuse*: name calling and denial of emotional needs.

Physical punishment feeds on itself especially if carried out when the adult is angry. The individual inflicting the punishment will have to continue to hit and hit harder and more often to bring about the desired behavioral changes. This is abuse. Children are not mature enough to make the necessary adjustment to make all the changes that are required of them to avoid punishments, so they develop ways to deal with what they consider to be unfair. They will lie, blame others, manipulate, and develop all types of defense mechanisms, because they simply can't win against authority figures.

Grownups who hit are continuing the cycle of violence in the home. Most of those who hit will tell you that they were hit as children and they turned out ok. The truth is: some children are hurt more by displeasing their parents than receiving physical punishments. Such a child you do not have to spank often. That is the good boy or girl. The *bad child* will eventually not care about being punished.

If you are hitting a child daily, something is not working. Obviously, physical punishment is not a deterrent to criminal behavior or the jails would not be so full of black youths. The jails are full of those who were beat often and hard.

I tell family, students, and clients that I do not believe in hitting children. I am an advocate of listening and reasoning.

Education has a number of **disorder classifications** that educators use when dealing with certain students. The school psychologist will test a child that has been observed displaying certain behaviors. However, most educators will not suggest you have your child tested because the school district would have to bear the cost of the assessment. Consequently, the aggressive parents generally get the testing that is needed. Generally, there is an assessment and classification of several disorders: **Behavioral Disorder** (BD) **Attention Deficit Hyperactive Disorder** (ADHD) and **ODD** (Oppositional Defiant Disorder), **Dyslexia** (a reading disability where letters move, rearrange, flip, or dissolve), and **Dyscalculia** (problems in conceptualizing math). The last of these is rarely recognized or discussed. A spectrum of other disorders can affect childhood learning.

To the layman, all of these classifications become overwhelming. In Adult Education, many adults have problems passing the math portion of the ABE or GED tests. I am empathetic because I simply cannot grasp certain concepts in higher levels of math: algebra, geometry, trigonometry, and calculus. I avoided most math classes until I had to take a statistics course in order to get an MA in psychological services. Math teachers teach to those who understand; the rest in class get a tutor or just do minimal work to pass. Most educators are not even familiar with dyscalculia and urge the student to study.

We must begin to recognize strengths and weaknesses. Challenges in one area should not preclude success in all. Advanced math requirements are going to wreak havoc with many educational plans. We need to recognize differences in learning styles and capitalize on those. In my statistics course at Atlanta University, I studied with a group of people on weekends and holidays. At the University of California, the administrators involved wanted to know why the high achieving black students were doing badly in their math classes while the Asian students were doing well. They discovered that the Asian students studied in groups. After engaging the black students to do the same, they did better in their math classes.

If your child is placed in a special education class, it is generally due to assessments that show either developmental or behavior challenges.

Developmental problems mean they have trouble with reading, with math, or in processing other types of behavior. Behavior related issues include: ADHD, BD, and ODD. I have heard parents call their children stupid and lazy. Some have tried to beat knowledge into them while others have tried to humiliate them into performing on grade level. Not understanding the nature of learning disabilities leads to frustrated parents who while good intentioned end up abusing their children. As soon as possible, the student drops out of school and becomes a dependent personality. These drop-outs learn to survive anyway they can. Most become depressive which leads to self medication and poly substance abuse.

Autism Spectrum is another classification in the DSM manual that is being diagnosed more and more. Autism is a spectrum. In other words, there are varying degrees of the disorder. Parents should look for symptoms such as: lack of social skills, minimal reaction to stimuli, lack of eye contact, a lack of intuition, lack of sympathy and empathy. Many autistic children have poor communication skills and are often socially awkward. They also display compulsive behavior, a tendency toward sameness, ritualistic behavior, restricted behavior. Those with the higher functioning Asperser's syndrome are seen as gifted in certain areas. It is my motivation to expose people to the possible causes of their child's behavior. People tend to seek simple solutions when their children act out or embarrass them. As we become more aware of the root causes and origins of certain behaviors we become more empowered to seek solutions. These solutions will be based in an understanding of the brain and how it functions.

The treatment of mental illnesses and the black community can go on for pages and pages. The disorders of schizophrenia, paranoia and the others not mentioned here should be researched carefully. Often more than one disorder can be observed in an individual. People with limited knowledge should not be reproducing because they simple do not understand the complexities involved in rearing children. A young teen mother or father cannot meet all the needs of a child. Often this child becomes a special needs child with many disorders created by the environment. The parent has not been trained to spot developmental problems in a child. Middle class parents are more aware of the needs of their children and more successful in addressing those needs. These parents are better advocates for their children.

Schizophrenia, Paranoid Personality, and Alzheimer related Dementia are more serious disorders. I have no expertise here and encourage those who are interested to research the types. Alzheimer issues needs serious attention to protect our aging population.

What Blacks Won't Say About Black Talk Radio

Listening to niche radio (ethnic or religious) with its targeted audience, one immediately notices how convinced the callers are of the authenticity of their station. Besieged by politicians, criminals, community, and family dysfunctions, authentic callers turn to the radio family. Talk radio is community radio, thus it reflects the tribalism of the patronizing consumer. To the advertiser who is seeking to attract and sustain a group of loyal consumers, the demographics don't matter.

In the South, the radio stations are overwhelmingly conservative. WSB AM had shock jock libertarian Neal Boortz who talked about welfare cheats and sluts. Neal even told one black caller that she and her ilk were too ignorant to vote. He made comments that women should be denied the right to vote. He got away with this because his producer/on air engineer, Marshall (now deceased), was black. His female banter buddy was a white female, Belinda, who feigned an *I-Don't—believe—you—said-that* sensitivity. They all were selling "stuff"(commercials) between the insults and politically incorrect attacks on everyone. As all good libertarians do, Neil challenged his audience on their attitudes toward the LGBT community. Boortz flew off in his plane leaving his empire to Herman Cain. As long as Herman continues satisfying the audience, with red meat comments when he is on air, he will prosper. That red meat being: taxes, failed policies, and far left educators.

I started listening to talk radio in the 60s in Detroit—specifically, Canadian Station (Windsor, Ontario) CKLW. It was neutral radio that instructed and enlightened. Ignorance was not tolerated. Civility was encouraged. Over the years, with a polarized political environment, talk radio has attracted an aging population of people who are losing their privilege and status. In imitating what works: limbaughesque radio has produced levin, savage, and beck radio. Rush Limbaugh is the de factor spokesman for the party: all genuflect except far western and northeastern GOP politicians. Talk radio is now as polarized. We have niche radio that reinforces the listeners' values. The advertisers just want to sell goods and services and increase corporate profits.

The programs are contrived. The repeated appearance—inclusion—of certain types of calls, and in some cases the same caller, makes it impossible for a discerning listener not to realize the screeners make sure the caller they want are the ones to be heard on the air. People tune in to listen to these people

Fred from Detroit, now living in Atlanta, describes himself as a conservative Republican and family man. He benefited from affirmative action and graduated from Michigan State. He expresses a high aversion to 'Gays' and lazy black people. The audience loves to hate Fred. He angers people with his Herb Caen-esque spiel. Fred's latest comments: all homosexuals sound gay. They have effeminate voices. He could tell that Mario, A regular caller, was gay when he heard him the first time. The attentive listeners think that Fred has to be a shill-a plant because he has all the talking points for the day on the president, lazy Negroes, immoral gays, liberals. Fred gets to out 'limbaugh' Rush and out savage Savage.

One of his equivalents in Detroit (Muslim and Afro-centric) believes that homosexuality like AIDS was introduced into the population by Europeans; that homosexuality is unknown in African culture. This caller continues that black gays are easily dismissed as white boys—Not to be taken seriously. Hostesses Mildred Gaddis in Detroit and Lorraine (white) in Atlanta challenge nonsense so as not to offend.

Mo Ivory, Atlanta, is more confrontational. The men on radio and television avoid extended discussions of taboo topics. In Atlanta, Derrick Boazman knows of no one concerned with marriage equality. In passing, he made a comment on Martin Luther King's gay aide chiding, "But y'all don't want to hear about that." Hosts know that some topics are taboo to black men. Al Sharpton is the one nuveau, Median-made, tele-news journalist who really does believe in civil rights for all. One gets the impression that the others are toeing the political line. This excludes formally trained tele journalists who are in a more mainstream environment. The testosterone drive, powerless, alpha male callers come across as haters. They are rude to female hosts. They are jealous and critical of President Obama as Big Dog. He doesn't have enough African Americans in his cabinet. He is too beholden to Jews, Latinos, Asians Ivy Leaguers, the LGBT community, big Hollywood, and Wall Street donors.

On the other hand, one hears from **Nicole,** the sister with arms akimbo, and HER no nonsense view of current events from popular media gossip to heavy politics. She speaks in "siesta" metaphor and hyperbole that others take literally. She mentioned that she wanted to investigate a business man who called. The business man in question took it as a threatening move. The business types who call talk about how they can set up companies to help "our own." They cite the buying power of the community. Those dollars should remain in the black community. An endless litany of platitudes follows.

As a humanist and share capitalist, I know that the color of your boss has little to do with anything. They all will pay you minimum wage. Pythagoras of the eponymous math theory posited centuries ago of 3 types of men:

1) **those of profit and gain;**
2) **warriors for glory and honor: gladiators, soldiers and modern athletes;**
3) **philosophers/ and** those into discovery (people to whom money and fame are not important).

The Lesson here is: the capitalist is going to exploit you. It's the name of the game. Color green of money is the bottom line.

Mario, a Clark-Atlanta University graduate, is extremely articulate. Mario is a journalist and confronts the audience on their fears. He is active in the LGBT community and articulates the "gay agenda" as simply one of equality for all. Mario is community oriented and cosmopolitan. Those callers with an aversion to LGBTs call and snipe. Since they "don't hate nobody" I will use *aversion to* in describing their remarks. Powerless men have an aversion to those things that are non tribal. As self-perceived leaders with strict roles for everyone, they have become anachronisms. Mario confronts them. He and Jason Collins are not looking for forced or token acceptance. Broussard of ESPN expresses a biblical view that will continue to be debunked. Broussard opines that gays are in open rebellion to his god-his deity.

Jihad, I consider him the Muslim, Alpha Male, Warrior, Afrocentric, homophobic. This caller uses all the classic arguments against *homosexuality*: It is a "deviant life style". He makes comparisons to all of society's sub-cultures. Jihad looks at nature and sees a natural order of things. And since we are not living according to the Koran we all shall perish. He is rigid and solipsistic.

On Atlanta's WAOK you hear **Bro Muhammad**: A Muslim, he is a screaming hypertensive. He presents himself as someone who is going to 'bust a vein' soon telling all the high and mighty bourgeois Negroes to take to streets to help their people. He greets with the Muslim greeting of Peace and Paradise and then goes into his hateful condemnation of everything. The lack of empathy, common in most men, limits them. I think it is genetic and environmental—chemical and cultural, an ignorance of hard science and social science.

Wayne (Atlanta) says there are only 2 professions: accounting and law. In college at Michigan the business types, pre law, pre med and engineers openly expressed that other majors were wasting a big ten education on literature, arts, and education. This attitude is prevalent among Pythagoras' men of gain and profit and black entrepreneurs.

The cast of callers compose a dysfunctional family. They run the gamut of family members from the crazy uncle to church lady. There are academics who call, but they are few. My academic friends don't know why I listen to talk radio. It is obviously contrived like the reality shows to increase market share for sponsors. The hour is less than 20% content: commercials and community service announcements abound. The stations are oriented toward Christians. Calls from Muslims and black Israelites annoy the Christian community of listeners.

An MBA friend of mine in Chicago says the callers just want to hear themselves talk; that they need to be at work or looking for a job. It's not that simply explained. Talk radio allows them to vent. The powerless and uneducated can get on air and express their frustration. They are losing control of everything. Nothing works: government, customer service, car maintenance, crime deterrents. There is an eroding of rights with another tribe getting preference. There is a preoccupation with material possessions and getting rich. Entrepreneurs see themselves in the affluent, leisure class and don't begrudge the 1%ers a thing.

Black talk radio is different from other talk radio only in that the participants see things in terms of them against the world because of their race. Some callers are hopelessly mired in talk about reparations and a unified pan African community.

Until the demanded reparations materialize, we must help one another and ourselves.

WHAT WE DO AND NEED TO DO

As blacks left the South and moved to the North and far west, they were able to live in lower and middle class homes in the industrial cities. Around Detroit, they were able to buy homes on the blue collar salaries that they were earning from working at the auto plants. The workers lived well and, for the most part, maintained those homes.

But what happened to that city, a city where people cared that much about their neighborhoods appearance? As blacks moved into the northwest neighborhoods of Detroit, middle and upper class of whites and Jews moved out to Southfield, Novi, and points northwest and west. As the 60's progressed, and blacks were beginning to want suburban home, a backlash occurred—the inevitable class of cultures: second generation immigrants of Poles, Italians and Jews against rural Southern blacks. The conflict continues: Coleman Young's fiery them-against-Us rhetoric created infamous city versus suburb on-going clashes. Blacks lived in the western suburb of Inkster and the environs of the airport but they couldn't move to Warren or Roseville (north-northeast of the city). 8 Mile Rd contained people of color to the South.

What Blacks Need To Say To Other Blacks About Their Neighborhoods

- **Don't buy a house on** overtime pay, small lottery winnings, or other **unreliable income**. During economic hard times, you will not have that extra income. Live within your means. Don't play that keeping-up-with-the-Joneses game. The Joneses are hurting like you are.

- **Maintain your house**: paint, pressure watch and make repairs to windows, doors, etc. The house we moved into on Richton ST in Detroit was in full decline. Paint was peeling, plumbing leaked, shingles literally dropping off. We never knew what the original color of the house was—green? gray? The brick houses withstood the harsh Michigan winters better.

- **Maintain your lawn/yard**: Plant flowers and trees, and keep grass cut. Learn how to do your landscaping if necessary. I offended a neighbor by cutting his grass. I did it as a favor. I did not expect payment because he was a good neighbor. He offered me barter which I refused. I concluded that it was pride. He did, however, begin to cut his grass more often.

- **Teach your family** members not to litter and DO pick up litter when you see it. As I jog, I carry a bag to pick up the litter. The biggest offenders are cigarette and blunt smokers, fast food eaters, single drink alcohol drinkers, and soda drinkers. Condom wrappers and candy wrappers are also common. The city does not have the manpower to attend to litter. I have never heard of anyone who has gotten a ticket for littering. My nephew threw a beer bottle out of my window when I told him he could not drink or smoke in my car. Obviously, it is acceptable behavior. The streets and highways are full of such litter. My number one annoyance (pet peeve) is the refusal of neighbors to pick up old circulars and papers from the driveway. A household of 5 or 6 people will walk by an advertising circular and not pick it up—not the adults, not the children.

- **Report** the houses involved in **illegal activity**. In some black neighborhoods, up to a third of the houses are involved in illegal activities: mostly drug sales. Some young families, who can rent a foreclosed home, sell drugs to make ends meet. They see nothing wrong with it. I suspect that a few of my neighbors sold or are selling drugs. The signs? Different cars of all types, BMW to pickups trucks and hoopties driving up and making transactions at the door. High class drug dealers are more discreet. The drug dealing exists on all levels.

- **Section 8 housing** is rented by people who have no property or investment interests. There is little oversight from the government agencies that place such individuals. We had a Section 8 problem that the neighborhood association had to confront: out of control youths, open drug use, slow destruction of the house, absentee guardians, etc. With the present sequestration and other budget cuts Section 8's future is not on sound footing. It places subsidized renters in areas with homeowners with vested interests. Most of my neighbors want it abolished. I don't know much about it, so I temper my comments.

- **Prevent the ghetto-ization** of your neighborhood. What are the signs? Young people walking in the middle of the street.

When the underclass moved from Detroit to Southfield (MI) the police had to tell them that they couldn't walk in the middle of the street and that they couldn't play basketball in the middle of the street. Another sign: loud music that shakes your house. You can hear them coming from blocks away. I called the police, and they told me to call them or take down a license number when it happened again. I don't see an easy solution to this one. Another sure sign: Kids hanging out on the corner calling each other niggas, bitches, assholes, faggots and motherfuckers—a total disrespect for everybody. Limit the number of convenience stores, liquor, stores and specialty stores for other vices

- especially porn. Middle class communities do not allow them.

- **Do not allow transient relatives** to move into your home who might cause problems for the neighborhood. Some homes are revolving doors for every dysfunctional family member. People will move in with a relative or friend who preys off children or any adult they can. You have a responsibility to your neighbors.

- **Stop chaining up your pets** to posts and trees. People with problem pets have made them so. The hyper masculine world of Michael Vick and dog fighting is common. A young black male was trying to goad a fenced in dog to fight his pit-bull. I have seen dogs languish and die while limited to a few feet of fenced space. I hear these animals howl through the night. An unleashed pit bull attacked my moving vehicle. Dog lovers will insist that their pets wouldn't hurt anyone. Let them be advised that their animals are friendly to them not to strangers; not to children who reach into their feeding bowl. Many vicious maulings of children and other animals occur too often.

- While most people consider old school block clubs and modern **neighborhood associations are necessary** evils, they protect common property investment interests. Remove old cars. Don't park on the grass. Bring in the garbage can when you get in or have the children do it. Respect the noise ordinance. Get the license plate numbers of the cars that are rocking your house with loud music and make police reports. You are allowed the quiet enjoyment of your home. I can hear some cars coming from blocks away.

- **Do random acts of kindness** for a neighbor. Take out or bring in the garbage can. Give them the names of reasonable handymen. Compliment their yard or house or car.

WHAT NEEDS TO BE RECOGNIZED IN THE BLACK CHURCH.

Religion is the result of men trying to explain the universe around them. Mythology provided reasons for the passing of the sun from horizon to horizon. The sun is generally carried across the sky by a god from sunrise to sunset. As for seasons, in Greek mythology a maiden Persephone had to be rescued from Hades annually to bring spring. It is extremely difficult to believe and accept rumors of miracles of today. Silhouettes of the Virgin Mary abound in everything from foods to the clouds. My point is: one cannot accept at face value the *miracles* of one's faith. Individuals with my perspective are baffled as old teachings and mythologies are passed on in religion.

The bible presents its own problems especially to a linguist. Material written millennia ago in arcane tongues, by scribes with limited vocabularies must be suspect. Scribes had limited vocabularies and many terms used cannot be translated. Beyond that, the nuances of a language are lost in any translation. For example: Spanish doesn't have a word for *ride*. They say *aventon* (favor) or *ree-day* (corruption of ride). Or, consider the words: stare, look, see, observe, and watch. Each has a slight different meaning which may or may not translate carrying the same meaning.

Beyond definitions, the phrasal nature of English (verb + preposition or adverb: come in, come over, come at, come through) carries a great deal of information which does not translate exactly. In short, the translations from Amharic (Jesus' language) through Hebrew or Greek or Coptic on into Latin languages and ultimately to the Slavic and Germanic languages such as English makes the translations highly suspect.

When I read the bible in French, Italian, or Portuguese, I see nuances in meanings; words and passages that can be translated in various ways. In that FAITH is more important than scholarship in the black community, little discovery is done on such issues. But the power of *the word* is unquestionable. All religious communities hold on to the *true faith* mantra maintaining that only through their particular ascetic can one be saved from a terrible fate in the afterlife. The damnation is so great that even the agnostics dare not risk not believing. If you question or don't believe, you face hell for eternity. Is this a compassionate God who forgives? More progressive believers tell me that this is metaphor.

And those even more progressive see hell and heaven as metaphors. I don't see greatly flawed leaders of the past who owned slaves, and treated their family member as chattel as one big happy family sharing milk and honey in heaven.

The Sunday morning rite is ubiquitous throughout the bible belt and Black communities around the country: urban, suburban, rural. Easter Sunday when everyone is welcomed and forgiven, as is the Christian fashion. The vilest of misanthropes: murderers, rapists, and thieves can repent on his/her deathbed and be received in the kingdom of heaven. All is forgiven OJ, Michael Jackson, Robert Kelly, Jayzee, Curtis Jackson, Ice Cube and Tea. Here we have the seed of societal and family dysfunction.

In the mega churches, Blacks follow the philosophies of their spiritual leader/CEO: the Eddie Longs, Creflo Dollars, and T.D. Jakes. The Creflo Dollar ministries are to me corporate structures. The pastor, as shepherd, reclaims those from sin (including homosexuality) through counseling. They don't hate the sinner; they hate the sin. The self hating, repressed Eddie Long has his New Birth Corporation. Blacks need to recognize the fact that these are corporate structures offering the perks of the business class: CEO status and its perks. As with the banks, there is sin forgiveness—too big to fail; to faithful to abandon. In congress, in church, in business the attitude is the same. My representative is OK; my pastor is OK. **We need to look in our own back yard.**

As with the selling of favors by the papacy, the Church has become a corporation that awards and punishes along class and economic lines. I am baffled by the ready acceptance by the peoples of Africa, Asia, and South America of the religions of Western Europe that destroyed civilizations and cultures from Alaska to Tierra del Fuego.

As Money is God in American Society, the Church is an on-going, self promoting money making enterprise. The church joins and teams with all financially successful entities and shares the profits. Religion. It is amazing that they don't see the money changers in the temple: the endless sales and fund raising activities. Should a shepherd tell the *sheeple* to invest in get rich schemes? "Of course, the Lord wants you to be prosperous." Not everyone can be rich. It's the pyramid of life: few on top and then the masses. Those vassals closest to the head will prosper in any structure.

The fact is our system is not based on socialistic principles. In capitalism, those who own the means of production, those at the top of the pyramid, will proper. Those lower in the structure usually wait for the excess trickle down crumbs. Everyone cannot become rich. Life is a hierarchy. Blacks are not familiar with economic system. They are only familiar with a free market type of capitalism based in what progressive European have labeled as a form of Anglo-Saxon exploitation—the amassing of wealth for wealth's sake.

In the black community there is nothing wrong with gross materialism, egoism, and crass avarice. The scriptures prescribe a life of pious modesty. There should be an eschewing of bravado (swagger) associated with sport, an eschewing of avarice associated with human desires. I like that Muslims don't believe in profit. In Buddhism there is no emphasis on the concept of sin; there is karma—you reap what you sow, what goes around comes around.

I asked someone in my family, who had condemned me to hell, what happens when I passed out from the fire and brimstone? I was told, "God will wake you up, and burn you some more, forever." Here is love?

Every presentation of facts will evoke vitriol from those who are very protective of their leaders. I do not have an issue with the church itself; as I want to be respected, I respect others. For some Faith is all they have. But, as I teach, absolute power corrupts absolutely. I am saddened to think that no amount of reading of the history of the Catholic Church and its popes (Borgia, in particular); of the Spanish Inquisition, The Reign of the Tudors (Henry VIII) etc. and the justification of slavery by the early American Protestants will change any views on the excesses of religion. I am reminded that there are theologians and then there are Church People. Church People have no need for theology. Theologians seek to keep church people with the stuff of true faith; with doctrine, with dogma. Theologians may or may not believe in the Bible literally; most see it as metaphor. Church folks see it as the "good book," and as such it is not to be questioned.

Use your intellect. Apply your rational mind to what you are participating in. If you still have your *faith* then please look at the institution you support. Blacks need to know that these are corporate structures offering the perks of the business class: CEO status and its perks. As with the banks there is sin forgiveness—too big to fail; to faithful to abandon. In congress, in church, in business the attitude is the same. My representative is OK; my pastor is OK. Look in your own back yard.

Women consider who is telling you to be quiet. Often you are carrying on the day to day work of the church, but you still have a limited role in the management of that church. Some of you are convinced that you should not have a leadership role in the daily running of church activities, but you do the true work. This is a familiar and sad dynamic. You take the translation you have been handed literally without consideration of the speaker (Paul not Christ) or the thousands of men who are still exerting power over you.

R E S P E C T: You demand respect for your beliefs, but dismiss and disrespect the faith of others. Those of other faiths: Muslims, Buddhist, Jews are not of the true religion and will not get into heaven. For the believer, all but you are heathens. You know very little of other faiths.

Do unto others . . . . Do not support forcing your practices on others. Mo Ivory (WAOK 1380 Atlanta) is going to pray for the atheists even if they don't want her to. In my professional life as a teacher, I have been shocked that black speakers at graduation and professional gatherings bring god into the arena. I asked a Jewish member of the school staff how she felt about these displays. The person I asked responded that it is inappropriate. Jews in the South have learned to be very discreet. I guess those of other religious groups have learned to accept or ignore what they hear everywhere. But this is not right.

MARRIAGE

I see marriage for what it is: a sociological institution. We hear much about the "sanctity of marriage". Historically marriage was a means of transferring ownership of a woman from her father to a husband. Procreation and property ownership were the goals.

Within the slave culture, blacks could not marry; they could only jump the broom. There was no coherent family unit. Members of a family could be sold off at any time. In slavery, anyone could be the father including the owner. By the time Negroes were able to have their unions accepted by the states, a pattern of loose sexual relationships had been long since a part of slave and post slave culture. Marriage, in the post slave society, would create a system of lineage.

However, we have a problem: not all men and, now women, are suited for marriage, yet many marry anyway, producing a male who will stray.

A large number of the male of the species are not monogamous. Nature tells me that; biology (hard science) tells me that. Religion serves to keep some men in line, but a male, generally, is not going to be faithful for very long. When he ejaculates, thousands of spermatozoa are dispersed (biology). On the other hand, the female has a finite number of eggs that she must use and use within a certain period of time. This scientific reality makes females somewhat less promiscuous. A man's natural drive is to mate. Religion wants him to "have a family" but what he does is breed. There are two men in Tenn. who have over 40 children between them—That's breeding. Society will not be able to sustain itself taking care of the children of the breeders. The children of the breeders commit more crimes and need more social services. They also use of more resources due to lack of education.

Marriage, I surmise, is intended for the good of females and their offspring. In the black community, before integration, you had shotgun weddings. If you got the girl pregnant you married her so that the child wouldn't be a bastard. Momma's baby, Daddy's maybe. The law is: those children born in a marriage are purported to be the sired by the husband. Someone has to take care of the children.

HOMOSEXUALITY

As a youth, I engaged in sexual experimentation with males and females in my age group. The famous Kinsey Report states that a large percentage of males engage in such activities with both sexes. It is often posited by the enlightened that those who show signs of homophobia are reacting to that childhood experimentation: or in Shakespearean parlance: *Me thinks thou doth protest too much.*

In the black community the *down low* (DL) male marries in order to hide his homosexuality. DL men are dependent on the largess of the community that does not accept their proclivities. They can be totally rejected. The icons in all areas of black society have made comments that condemn same sex attraction. Science: one portion of the brain of heterosexual females and male homosexuals is similar. Correspondingly that part of the brain is similar in Lesbians and straight. Homosexuality is genetic for the most part.

Those without an appreciation for science over faith will not understand that no one would choose to be *like that*. Eddie Griffin in his comedy act says, "Ain't nobody proud of a gay son." Magic Johnson's comment on his son was helpful in neutralizing gratuitous remarks. Rapper Ludicrous calls Bill O'Reilly a "faggot" when he addresses his lyrics. Isaiah Washington calls a cast member a "gay slur" when he is late for their top rated medical show rehearsal. Kobe Bryant calls a courtside official a gay slur, but he supports Jason Collier. Family Feud host, comic, and author Steve Harvey got in trouble for using a slur years ago. The Rutgers coach humiliated his players calling them the worst names for sissy boys. Fred, local talk radio caller, calls Ronald Reagan's son a sissy. A minister says of a boy given to criminal behavior at church: "At least he's not a faggot." The worst thing you can be in the black community is homosexual or atheist. They are worse than child molesters. These types of comments are one reason you have men marrying who should not be marrying. If you are dependent, without a job, or a place to live, you must shelter those behaviors from those who are taking care of your immediate needs.

EDUCATION

Speaking, reading, and writing English are difficult. Speaking, however, allows for more flexibility. The non reader's ear does not distinguish certain sounds. 'Could've' and 'would've' sound like 'could of 'and 'would of'; effect (noun) and affect (verb) are used interchangeably—and that is somehow acceptable. As we become more and more a society of non readers, the spoken language will become even more fluid than it is now—corruptions will be allowed: fishes(fish), shrimps(shrimp), the media is (are), the man was laying (lying) on the ground. Newsreaders are just as guilty, even though they have writers and editors.

In analyzing the problems with English communication, I have developed my own non scientific system of English fluency: Lower classes communicate from 20-30% fluency. This speech is for communication and object acquisition. It is laconic and mostly monosyllabic. Their speech has few grammatical rules and is full of the latest cultural colloquialisms. "Wassup" is a greeting. "Chillin'" is the response; and "gettin my eat on," or ". . . work out on," is elucidation. When confronted with grammar/pronunciation the response is "don't nobody talk like dat."

Thirty-Fifty% speakers can communicate well enough to hold certain jobs but are limited by presentation, surly appearing responses, and the bringing of cultural adornments (bling, tattoos) to work. These speakers might be high school graduate in urban or rural areas. Those at the **50 %** fluency can speak the language but choose to use dialect. They can make subjects and verbs agree and know most of the irregular forms of plurals. They also enunciate at a comprehensible level. Some are people in positions of leadership who leave written communication to their secretaries and read their speeches. Language to them is a brain function that is beyond them. And I am not so sure that they don't have a point. Studies have shown that females are much better at language due to centuries of social evolution. Women sat around talking while men were out hunting making arcane sounds to each other.

Those at high level of fluencies, **60 to 70%** are professionals who have a facility for the spoken language. This facility may or may not translate into reading or writing skills. English speaking academics are at the highest level. They know the different between a transitive verb and an intransitive verb. They can spell (due to memory and practice); can distinguish the past participle from the past tense; know the plurals of words from Greek and Latin; and CAN make a subject and verb agree using indefinite articles. They know how to use amount, fewer, a number of, a minority of, etc.

The problem here is that the individual who is speaking the language at **less than 50%** proficiency is not going to get the job. When I am teaching language, young black people say to me, "Don't nobody talk like dat (that)". The problem also seems to be related to gender. Males, and especially black males, have a poor grasp of the language. Derrick Boazman, former Atlanta councilman and now radio host, breaks every grammatical rule; so much so, I think it has to be for effect. This speech has no agreement of subject and verb; malapropisms abound, and the confusion of past tense and past participle is ubiquitous: I have went (gone); I have came (come); I have ran (run). Is the acceptance of bad grammar from black media personalities intentional? Or, do they speak in this manner for effect? Have they imposed acceptance of the fact that correct usage doesn't matter?

My reasoning is this: **You can't tell young black males to succeed by educating themselves and then continue to split verbs and mispronounce words.** Males don't learn if you preach to/at them; they learn by emulation and imitation. Icons such as Al Sharpton can make egregious mistakes (crisis=crisises (crises); accents on wrong syllables, malapropisms, etc. The sycophants of the men that I will mention will take issue with what I am saying. No one is allowed to criticize the icons of the black community. They will say that I am a black man attacking other successful black men; that I am jealous; that language does not matter when making money—men don't listen for grammar. All True—but poor language offers limitations to those leaving the lowers classes. Since speaking the language correctly has been effeminized and made "a white thing, it is not a priority. Don't the younger sports commentators get training in using standard usage? I don't think those in charge of delivery and presentation would tell these men to "SPEAK ENGLISH!" Judge Joe Brown and Kwame Holliman (NPR) Eugene Robinson, Dr. Cornell West and Tavis Smiley speak English.

- **Corrections**: I want to yell at the television/radio/speaker. I *have* come; I *have* gone; I *have* begun; I hurt (past tense—not hurted); I spread (not spreaded). I *have* run, I *have* seen. Or, as Mildred Gaddis (WCHB Detroit) says: "There is a word between I and gone, I and seen," etc. I have gave—*NEVER!* The words brung, costed, flang (fling) or hitted (hit) do not exist. Busted may be acceptable in the spoken colloquial meaning for arrested, but the past tense of bust is burst. *The balloon burst.*
- The **double negative**: "Don't nobody know." "Aint nobody got no time for that never."

- **Plurals**: deer (no deers) moose (no mooses) fish (fishes has a more rarefied meaning than the plural of fish) NEVER sheeps, or shrimps or childrens or gooses. People's women's and men's are possessives forms not plurals. Many demonstrate a total avoidance of the Latin words that end in 'us': cactuses is ok, cacti is better. 'Crises' is the plural of crisis, NEVER crisises. And every grammarians least favorite: 'the media is"—ugh!!! This misuse is UBIQUITOUS from BBC to local *newsglib* and *glamourglib*.

- **Subject verb agreement**: The use of "I is," "you is," or "they is," and the corresponding past tense use of "you was," "we was," "they was" is unacceptable. The use of the indefinite pronouns (none, one, some, a majority, a number, etc.) with the incorrect verb form abounds.

- **Verb usage**: Only those speaking at 90% fluency know how to use the non-countable 'amount': amount of water—yes," amount of people-no. 'Fewer' (countable) and 'number' (countable) fall into the same regular misuse. Even the BBC and NPR falter with transitive and intransitive verbs such as lay/ lie, shine (shoe as opposed to a light), and hang (a person and an object).

I heard on the BBC the other day that the American Dream is a lie, but everyone buys into it. Young black men are told they will be successful if they: go to school, work hard, keep their noses clean, and make money. The fact is human civilization has favored a pyramid societal structure: A ruler or autocrat on top, a smaller class with access to the top (vassals and power seekers) and the masses below. Consequently, only so many people are going to make it to the top. The masses will spend their lives in the struggle that is survival. Human existence is basically varied forms of slavery; now it is debt. Earlier, slavery was literally people as chattel property. Greek and Roman societies were built by slaves as well as North America, South America and the Caribbean. In order to escape from the lower classes, one has to have connections or certain abilities valued by the society. Morehouse at one time was turning out marketing majors who never found jobs. The NCAA schools are turning out athletes who can't talk, write, or manage money. The pyramid has to be sustained. Too many people cannot be allowed at the top.

The college degree once was a discriminator assuring mastery of language, certain knowledge, and trainability. The degree no longer offers passage to the middle class or higher. While attending Atlanta University (1987-90), I learned to accept that most of my fellow students were getting degrees to make more money, and the University was in a type of pact with them to grant them degrees. Students did not buy books, did not come to class, and did not have intellectual pursuits. I was so disgusted at the process that I never picked up my degree from Atlanta U. I guess it is still there. I thought I was attending the intellectual institution of DuBois et al. I ended up making money rewriting papers making subject and verbs agree on theses for students on all levels.

In order to be relatively financially secure in American society, black men will have to excel at the academic level. There is nothing new in the fact that there are only so many spots on national sports teams. People's first impressions are of your carriage and your speech—there is nothing else to go on. Money can be made in the trades, but those are not positions of power that men tend to aspire to.

Men of influence in the community need to speak the language properly. It is not a question of "do as I say, not as I do." Men emulate other men. If powerful black men who have exposure to young black men had better speech, or made comments on the importance of good speech, we would see change. They should be made aware of the importance of presentation and other intangibles: empathy and body language, in particular.

The School Board

In the cities where I have worked, I encountered the same racial politics shared by all big city systems: race, immigrant population, gender, shrinking tax base, teacher salaries and strikes, affluent vs. poor and transient communities, superintendent and school board issues. The abuses of the school board are many. Large black districts are not worse; they are just indiscreet with their misconduct, malfeasance, and nepotism.

I have worked for Detroit Public School, Oakland Unified School District, Fulton County Schools(GA.), Marietta City School(GA), and Cobb County Schools(GA). I looked at the Clayton County School District (GA) application and found it to be inappropriate, so I never submitted it. I could not get employment at Atlanta Public Schools or DeKalb County Schools (predominately black districts). In those systems, I was told that I needed to know someone or be related to someone (nepotism).

In Detroit in the early 60's-70's, the school district was changing and young minority teachers were hired into high schools as part of affirmative action and other programs. Many of the white teachers had moved to the suburb and therefore were not eligible for promotions due to residency rules: those who didn't have Detroit zip codes could not be promoted. In Oakland, the racial/class problem was highlands (expensive homes) vs. lowlands (poor/immigrant). In metro Atlanta, the conflict comes in the form of the southern part s of the counties vs. the northern parts of Fulton, DeKalb, and Cobb counties. In the cities of Marietta and Atlanta, it is homeowners vs. apartment dwellers.

Recipe for School Failure

The failure of the schools looms as a reason for the decline of urban areas. As with any corporation that is the major employer in an area, school boards are political entities that serve their stakeholders.

Characteristics Of Urban School Boards

- **Largest employer in county**
- **Contact and familial relationships are important**. In Detroit, I asked for a social worker. I was amazed at how she could pick up the phone, explain my situation to her friends and get me a job. In my case, the professional contacts helped me a great deal. However, many people hold powerful positions for which they are not qualified or should be dismissed but can't be due to their contacts.

  Boards have members without education in or exposure to other cultures. Many boards do not have minimum education requirements, so you have people on school boards without any knowledge of the social sciences that govern human interaction. Some members don't believe in, sociology, psychology, science (evolution in particular), or educational theory and practices. Nor do they believe in the separation of church and state. They want prayer back in the schools. Some board members have brushes with the law and terrible financial backgrounds that should preclude their taking on such responsibilities.

In Oakland, the black community was indifferent to or outright hostile to the immigrant communities. When I told one of my administrators that the black kids were bullying the Asian and Latino kids, he informed me that they needed to know abuse and discrimination. In the 90s, I watched the Atlanta School Board meetings on local cable. It was farcical: the same old racial recrimination and faux displays of being insulted by adversaries—usually white.

Highly Coveted Construction Contracts are meted out along arcane rules. The result: corruption. DeKalb County and Clayton County are recent school boards in trouble for such practices. DeKalb lost its Superintendent for such suspect actions. Many school boards are criminal enterprises waiting to be caught.

- **Testing Programs** are run by administrators looking for favorable results and bonuses. Atlanta Public School has proven the worst offender of late, but this could be any school district large or small. A quality education means more than doing well on tests, and teaching is a lot more than is more than teaching to the test by using technology. It is more than after school activities and tutoring. I don't test well. I did not get into Emory because I didn't test well. I avoided classes in college that required testing. I stuck with instructors in the social sciences and languages. I am a social scientist. While I do not have an aptitude for math or science, many people with those abilities lack my aptitude for language.

Self

What Works For Me

There are certain principles that I have adopted that help me avoid the tribalism and social cannibalism of a given culture or subculture. Those who emerge with some degree of sanity from their rearing have done so because they have managed to adapt to the current mainstream culture. Asians are expert at it. And Jews excel at adapting and assimilating to mainstream while maintaining cultural traditions. Education is paramount in all groups.

First generation children are always "tweeners" (between cultures). They want to dance, dress, talk, eat, smoke, *sin* (not in my lexicon) as their peers do; however, you will not see Asian and Jewish youth sagging (underwear and or butt showing). Black middle class kids will sag; wear crazy head gear and bling' (excessive adornments) but only after they leave the house in the morning. Many have told me that dad or mom did not play that foolishness: that they would not be wearing exotic hairdos, body etchings, or bling when a parent might see. In short, there is something about black youth culture that encourages more in-your-face rebellion and mockery of the larger society. I do not see excessive jewelry or body piercings/tattoos in those communities with these historically rigid cultures.

It can be said that the culture of the "American Negro" is modern in that the ties with traditional African culture is superficial and romanticized at the same time. Blacks from the States are the most Americanized of all groups: the ultimate consumer of everything American from designer shoes to luxury items they cannot afford. Most of them believe in the American Dream. Those from Africa and Europe know that the Dream is a fantasy—a lie, a myth, a paradox, etc. People around the world who have dealt with needs versus wants know that we North Americans have confused the two and our wants have become needs. This consumerism was spreading to the world quickly before the collapse (2008). China, Brazil, and Singapore will be upcoming excess stories.

Fact is there are few needs: food, oxygen, air, shelter. Big Screen TVs, trips to casinos, designer this and that on infants, pianos that you can't play, etc are not essentials or needs. First generational high income is spent on those things that identify you are having arrived—the appearance is more important than actually having the possession. The old British comedy "Keeping up Appearances" is a perfect example. Hyacinth, while comfortably middle class, gives candlelight suppers, test drives expensive cars, and wants to buy a country estate on her middle class husband's salary. She eschews everything about her humble, middle class origins which include her ribald sister, Rose, and her n'er-do-well brother-in-law. "Daddy" is a bit eccentric and lives in a fantasy world of World War II adventures. "Daddy" is a flasher and a masher too. She reminds everyone that she does have a sister who has a Mercedes and lives in a fashionable part of town. Her son, never seen, is obviously gay, and hits her up for a few pounds every now and then. Her husband is a long suffering English gentleman. The die is cast for the

North American version of those aspiring to the leisure class of privilege. Excess (used to be rising middle class income and home equity) created wants that became needs that fueled consumerism—must—do's and must—have's in capitalism.

What I Intimate To Those Struggling

Celebrate as few holidays as you can. I am conflicted about many holidays, so I do not celebrate any. The consumer nation moguls have a plan to get your money. There is a not so subtle plan for you to spend. New Years Eve/Day is for entrepreneurs who make their money selling drink, food, and party favors.

Martin Luther King Day has been disrespected by being commercialized with sales. And they scream at you during the advertisements. In the black community you will find concerts or Church services. Church services mean passing the collection plate many times or going to see the clergy for prayer. Those who are less reverent will find an excuse to do anything. It is a 3 days weekend. Most people go to work. It is a holiday for black people as Columbus Day is for Italians and St Patrick Day is for the Irish.

Then there is **Presidents' Day**: sales and programs. Besides, how can I celebrate a slaver? George Washington owned Slaves freeing two personal servants at his death. Some historians say that Jefferson freed his slaves while others say he didn't because freedmen had nowhere to go in Virginia at that time. These people were his children by Sally Hennings. As to other slaves, he waited until he died to free them and by then was so in debt that his heirs did not free all he intended. The apologist, among those historians, will tell you that he felt really badly about owning slaves; that he was a man of his times. Lincoln was ambivalent about freeing the slaves. He simply wanted to preserve the

Union. Mr. Lincoln did not consider Negroes to be equal to whites. He knew that they would never be accepted as equals. Abe thought that they should be sent back to Africa or the Caribbean.

Valentine's Day is the money maker for florists, chocolatiers, card makers, and jewelry folk.

Income Tax Refund Day (unofficial floating holiday in black community). I discovered how poor people were affording big screens and other big ticket items. I either pay taxes or get little back in refunds. Poor people get big refunds and purchase their fantasy wants. An inmate student told me that his mother obtained all her "nice things" during tax refund season: TVs, cars, clothes, vacations, appliances.

Then the Irish holiday, **St Patrick's Day, Mothers and Fathers Days, Memorial Day, Fourth of July, Labor Day, Columbus Day, Veterans Day, Thanksgiving Day, Christmas Day** (the biggie). Black people go into debt from Christmas to Christmas. My mother, back in the 50's, would spend her $18 a week, earned from her maid job, buying Christmas toys that we would tear up. That tradition of splurging at Christmas is still strong. Parents were not good parents if they did not give the children a "good Christmas."

In short, holiday celebrating is not priority to me. They are all family days if I am in the mood for family activities.

- **Debt**: I don't buy clothes or anything new unless it's an appliance. My sisters and nieces think I should look a certain way, so they buy my clothes. I now shop at the Goodwill stores. I make purchases when I have enough money to pay for them or to make a sizable down payment. At this time, I need a new oven for my stove. I also need a refrigerator. I don't have an ice and water dispenser on my old one. I will purchase these items when I have the cash or almost all the money needed. Debt is the new slavery. Some form of slavery will always be with us. You can choose your master these days. I do like nice cars that will start. Every economy car I had failed on me after the warranty was up. That generally doesn't happen with high end vehicles.

- **Utilities**: I use very little heat or air conditioning. Most people's homes are too cold in summer and too hot in winter. My heat is kept at 62 degrees in winter and 82 in summer. I have conditioned myself to the heat and the cold. I do that by jogging in the day in warm weather (under trees) and in winter, I jog in minimum running clothes. Luckily, in Georgia you can jog daily with a mean high temperature of 51 degrees in January and a sultry 89 or 90 in summer. I pay only $150 a month for utilities. I do splurge on my smart phone. I do everything on my smart phone. Most of this book was written on phone. In winter I see few people on the streets walking or running in black neighborhoods; same in the heat of summer. The energy wasted in poor people's homes is great. 15-30 minutes showers, thermostats set too high or too low. Windows and door opened with children going out and in.

- **Groceries/Food**: Poor people let their children eat as much as they want. In my family had beans daily and chicken on Sundays in the 50s and 60s. Many people from that generation have not gotten over the hunger pangs. Like Scarlett O'Hara, they will never go hungry again.

Overeating and the resulting obesity is a serious problem in all minority communities with Blacks and Hispanics being the most overweight. Grave consequences are being seen especially with females in the black community. Obesity is more accepted in the culture. Food and lots of it is everywhere. I was astounded that a lady brought and sold dinners at a teachers' workshop presented in the city. Diet presents one of the most difficult problems to address because food plays an important part in all cultures. We use food for many purposes other than nutrition. Church and funeral functions are replete with ample spreads of food and drink.

Advertising on black radio has seductive advertising for soul and fast foods. The fare is laden with cholesterol, fats, sugars, and disease causing additives, all at cheap prices. This ease of obtaining unhealthy amounts of food has created a group of people that will require unsustainable medical cost to address at a later date. Changing lifestyle choices is difficult. I am convinced that foods have been treated with flavor enhancements. Since I rarely eat fast food, the taste is attention getting. Since I rarely use sugar or salt, my taste buds are titillated by the first bite or sip of fast food. It is fun and addictive.

I have not seen my young nieces and nephews when they were not eating. And yes, they are putting on weight. Studies show that most parents don't see their kids as having a weight problem. They see it as baby fat; they will outgrow it. How do you tell them that the seeds of diabetes and other chronic illnesses are being planted now? I eat to kill hunger. I don't even budget for groceries. The community has come a long way but black professionals should present facts about diet to the forefront.

The refrigerators of my family members are so full that you can't get anything in them. Their status comes from having steaks and expensive cuts of meat in the freezer. I spend about $25 a week in groceries. I buy fish and chicken on sale. I know where to buy what. I use coupons and the sale papers. Some people spend $200 a week for groceries. I don't think they ever thought about making adjustments. Others spend lots of money on beer and wine. Lifestyle changes are the most difficult to make.

We have an obesity problem in the black community. My personal observation is that children are constantly eating. Most kids are always eating or drinking. Blacks spend a larger share of their income on groceries. The children, even poor ones, are obese because the parents see food in terms of quantity. They want their children to be full since these parents probably went hungry as children. The higher classes are more concerned with quality of food: fruits, vegetables, low sugars and fat; juices instead of corn syrup concoctions. Immigrants don't believe there is true hunger in America because they don't see emaciated people about in the streets.

Some Facts And Commentary To Share

- Eat smaller portions and stop eating when full. My brain sends signals that I am full after a few bites. I have weighed 150 lbs most of my adult life. (5'7, 32" waist)
- Eat out less thus saving money and excess calories (learn how to count calories
- Stop rewarding with candy (I was guilty of this).
- Cut out the southern country breakfast

Since I have a real problem with the pay of the workers at food service places, I minimize my visits. In these establishments, the young people work for 'wants' but older people work out of need. Both are exploited at fast food places.

- **ENTERTAINMENT**: I spend less than average on satellite TV. I manage to negotiate with the provider. I can't imagine buying or renting a movie. I will not spend money on a DVD or CD. I think most people have learned that there are only a few good tracks on any given CD. They download by single. The last time I went to a movie (2008), the people were so rude with cell phones and profanities that I decided not to go again. The prices for concert tickets and athletic events are prohibitive. Most people can't afford the stadiums their tax money helped finance. I will not patronize the likes of the team owners who get billions in revenue from worldwide distribution. This is something personal. Cities continue to finance the GAMES for the Fanatics. And the Fanatics come spending hundreds of dollar for a day at the Arena.

Minimizing My Wants Works For Me.

If you can't distinguish your needs from your wants you will forever be a slave to credit and its many forms. Clark Howard and other consumer advocates warn about the pitfalls of using credit for purchases made to satisfy wants. While credit is necessary, those who use credit wisely will encounter fewer problems living within their means. Household finances are a question of income and expenses. You can't spend more than you make. Unexpectedly expenses must be balanced with cuts in others areas: grocery, entertainment, clothes, etc.

Most women would not be comfortable in my kitchen because I only have a few skillets and pans. I buy sugar and salt maybe once a year. I used to buy "stuff" because it was on sale.

I do not attend ceremonies and rituals: weddings, funerals, graduations. I do not celebrate holidays. I do not wear jewelry unless you consider a watch jewelry: no bracelet, no rings, and no chains. I rarely entertain. I am working on becoming a minimalist. WHY? A stress free life comes from distinguishing your needs from your wants and from being strong enough to take the criticism from people who always want to give you advice. Another way of looking at it is after you examine how things are going you make changes because the unexamined life is not worth living—Socrates

EVOLVING THE NEGROES

In counseling others, professionals in the fields of psychology are taught not to give advice. The listener (counselors, psychologists, social workers, physicians/psychiatrists) should attend—that is, listen while acknowledging that the client is being heard. There is a professional pose/stance/position that is standard. The position of the body indicates that the mental health professional is empathetic. Also, the head is tilted toward the client and the arms are placed in a non threatening way near the knees of the listener.

Surprisingly, we are trained NOT TO GIVE ADVICE. I have incorporated this aspect of counseling into everyday interactions on all levels. Personally, people are always giving me advice: medical and otherwise. I was told to use antibiotics for a virus; take vinegar for high blood pressure; eat foods that I am allergic to; shop at a certain place; use corporal punishment on a child; do certain things for an interpersonal problem. Friends are always giving friends advice about how to deal with a certain individual at work of in interpersonal relationships.

If people see that your life is relatively drama free, and you have had some successes, those people around you will seek advice. Again, it is not wise to give advice. The client comes to choose a path toward a solution by the listener restating what the client has said. Ex: I hate my boss, my family member, my teacher, my mate. Restated: I hear that your boss, etc., makes you angry. I hear you saying your teacher doesn't like you.

The listener does not advise the client to confront the boss or the teacher. The client comes up with some possible solutions. The counselor can offer options or share similar experiences or situations.

Of course, the mental health professional needs to discourage or report situations of imminent danger by pointing our consequences of violent or illegal acts. It is understood that there is professional-client confidentiality at all times. All the aforementioned clarified, I find license here to actually give advice. It is a contradiction, but again, this is a direct appeal for some uniformity amusement and/or entertainment sake. To wit:

- **Expand Horizons** (the most important): Learn about another culture, subculture, society that you have an aversion to (prejudice). If you have friends of another race, gender/sexual orientation, profession, etc., you are more likely to see those people as not so very different from yourself. People within your own group give you the most problems. White on white or black on black or Latino on Latino crime is more common than intra-tribe/group crime (within that race). Inter-tribal exists, but those cases feed prejudice. "Those black thugs violated that elderly white couple." "Those Latinos attacked the South Central Los Angeles blacks who have been there for years." "Skinheads and Nazis and Klaners are attacking all minorities."

I used to see race. When growing up in segregated Rutherford County Tennessee of the 50's and 60's, everything was seen in terms of Negro/Colored and White folks. Blacks and Whites did not see a man on the corner. They saw a white or black man on the corner. If someone passed you in a car, you noted the color of that person. It was hard for me not to see color. We had to go upstairs at the Princess Theater in Murfreesboro, TN. We could not go to Shoney's or check into motels or hotels. I went to the Limbaugh Library, but no one every turned me away. I went to the packing house for pork parts for my science experiments, but the people in charge always gave me a lung, kidney, or heart. When I told my mother and grandmother, they thought I was crazy. "Boy, you can't go there; we colored," they laughed and shook their heads.

We had an upright piano in the corner of the living room that I used to bang on. I wanted piano lessons, because Miss Cotton, the music teacher, had infected me with a desire to play a musical instrument. We couldn't afford a flute or saxophone, so I would have to settle for playing the piano, if I could get someone to pay for lessons. Miss Cotton was too expensive at $2 an hour. Momma did find Rev. Francis at 50¢ an hour. There was some controversy about Rev. Francis. Although he was married, he acted like a "sissy". My siblings were furious. They wanted to know why Momma was wasting money on piano lessons, when the money should go to buy groceries. They figured and I knew that they had to get me out of the SOUTH, because I was too different and the environment was stifling me.

I left the segregated South in 1964 during the civil rights movement and subsequent sit-ins of the period. In Detroit, I went to integrated but tracked level classes. White students were more likely to be in college prep classes, blacks in "business" classes. Ironically, whites were nice to me and blacks were cruel. I call it the Clarence Thomas syndrome: People of any group may be meaning to you, but living well if the best revenge. In Georgia, Justice Thomas benefited from affirmative action as I did, but the white community would not let you forget race, and the black community would not let you forget that you were different: an outsider, a "tweener," a nerd.

You were accused of trying to be white for making subject and verbs agree and putting "eses" and "gee's" "g's" at the end of your words and using polysyllabic words. The Tribe was brutal to Justice Thomas and me because the members never sought to expand their horizons. The black kids laughed at my Southern accent and called me County Tennessee. My grandmother's sister's children (the closest I had to blood relatives in Detroit) thought me a country novelty. At school, I was identified as more teachable than the other middle schoolers and received positive attention from the white teachers. I had only one black teacher, the typing teacher. She had a Southern accent, so I avoided her, because the kids made fun of her too.

As a result of all this rejection, I retreated into a world of books as did Justice Sotomayor when she encountered a sterile environment. I did not leave the house much. I went to the library taking out books in Spanish, because I had discovered Spanish on late night stations of 50K watts. In college, a black classmate asked me why I was studying that white man's language (Spanish). It was that period of black racial consciousness of the 60's. There were no blacks in advanced Spanish classes. However, there were blacks in Italian classes: instrumental and voice music majors had to take Italian.

My exposure to whites and foreign students on campus made me more amenable to cultural differences. There was David C. from Nigeria. As a result of this exposure, I am more accepting of "foreigners." My Physician's Assistant now is a female Nigerian. My dentist is Brazilian with Middle Eastern origins. My best friends are Latinas and white females. I communicate with black males on a sports level or in the capacity of teacher in the prison system (my next book). Many blacks transferred to the School of Education to avoid of the language requirement at Michigan. Some asked me to take their exit Spanish exam to get degree from School of Literature, Science and the Arts.

- Consequently, I advise everyone to **read,** to **learn a language**, and to **cultivate friends from other groups**. I have always carried bags or books with me in my valise or briefcase. It was always bulging with books and magazines for the benefit of my nieces and nephews. To my disappointment, my nieces and nephews were not into books. WHY? There were very few books in their homes. Now that they are adults, they have books in their homes, and they tell their kids to be like UNCLE. "Uncle don't do nothing," they add. "Look at his hands. They are not calloused like mine, and he gets to sit on his ass all day and do nothing. He is like Tommy on Martin Lawrence's Show, he ain't got no job." This is a family joke.

I give the great grand nieces and nephews my smart phone and teach them to research or download. I know they will do games and inappropriate things on YOUTUBE. My oldest grand nephew, Q, gave me a book on Greek Philosophers this spring that he had taken out of the Limbaugh Library. It made my day.

My niece, Libby, is getting a minor in Spanish. And my nephew, Terrion, is on the Dean's list. He now writes me using complete sentences and vowels. I was not put off by his textscript with consonants only. I told him that Hebrew, Arabic and Farsi were generally not written with vowels. Now, if I can stop him from the "Sir" stuff . . . .

- **Seek new types of knowledge**: the sciences, hard and soft. I don't know if the eschewing of the hard and social sciences is a regional thing or an ethnic thing or both. Southerners tend to reject the theory of evolution and embrace creationism. The Earth is thousands of years old and was created by intelligent design (God).
- Personally, I have never understood how the oppressed can take on the gods of their oppressors. If I were in Africa, and was conquered by Arabs or a neighboring tribe, I would keep my own gods while appearing to take on Islam. When the Catholic Kings (Isabella and Ferdinand) ran the Moors (Muslims) from Spain in 1492, the Jews had to convert or suffer the consequences. The Jews maintained their religious traditions but appeared to be Catholic. The ancient Romans allowed their conquered foes to keep their gods, however, they rendered unto Caesar his tribute and taxes. The Bible reinforces that and has come to mean do what you need to serve the powers that be but give your deity your loyalties and devotion: "Render unto Caesar . . ."

My interpretation of sociology (social science) says to me that there has to be an orderly society with values and customs that ensure the perpetuation of the group. It appears that the more exploited and marginalized a people are, the more they cling to faith. In the brutal times of any slavery from the forms of Brazilian slavery under the

Portuguese to the North American version of eradication of family, language, native customs, etc., under the Brits, Scots, and Irish, the *godless heathens* had nothing but Master's God to deliver them. Blacks were bred scientifically (genetics) for success in the Americas. The late Howard Cosell got into trouble for saying so. To paraphrase him: They would breed the physically superior to get a specimen. The Native peoples of the Americas could not take the conditions and as a result died out from disease or grinding hours of labor in the tropical and subtropical sun.

From this history comes the root of modern *Negro* society. A society where the clergy is on top of the pyramid followed by shallow distinctions such a skin color: redbone, yella, high yella, light skinned and physical ability (prowess at sport). White society has evolved from that, but blacks are slower in making a transition to a meritocracy based on education. With knowledge of the sciences, I am able to analyze and come up with a prescription for life that works for me. I simply cast off all that does not pass tests for good reason and logic.

- The social sciences, psychology, sociology and even theology explain the interconnectedness of society and expected behaviors. For years, all societies have participated in ceremonies and rites that have been traditions. We as humans (social primates) are programmed and indoctrinated with beliefs that we don't question. For the majority of people, many of these drives are innate and cannot be stifled. As a result, the individuals who do not share in these beliefs and/or drives who suffer the consequences of societal pressures to marry and produce.

Public Personae/ Why Do You Do That In Public?

- **Smoke weed or cigarettes**. Young blacks will light up anywhere. It's illegal. I am of the Libertarian school of thought: Drugs should be legalized and their sales regulated by the government. Cannabis, synthetic drugs, and pills are illegal. Their possession will get you jail time. You should not drive around with contraband, especially if you are in the car with people with warrants. Don't drive with expired tags, or defective lights. Once you become a part of the prison industrial complex, it is hard to extricate yourself.

- **Rocking the block** with super AMPS (loud music). When I was in my 20's, I used to blast my music to the displeasure of the young lady who lived above me in Detroit. Now it is Karma time. I do not have quiet enjoyment of my home because drivers come by with their music blaring vibrating the whole block. You can hear them coming in their hoopties (old cars) with rims (more valuable than the car). The music awakens you in the middle of the night. In traffic, such music drowns out the sound of my talk radio. Old folks listen to talk radio. "Play your music for yourself," I was always taught. Those thumping and bumping with loud bass shows a lack of respects for others. Not much you can do about it. The police can't ticket them all. In addition, if you don't know better there is nothing you can do with people in their 30's and 40's who do the same. REMEMBER, music preference varies greatly—it is a private thing. There are programs on radio and TV for those with esoteric musical taste. I turn off all interviews of musicians and singers. I don't watch any award show. If it is not classical, jazz, R&B or New Age, I don't listen to it. And I assume that others prefer rap, country, rock, metal, etc. Music is personal taste I don't want to hear your noise, especially if it is hollering at me about bitches, hos, sluts, nigga, and fags.

WHERE TO LOOK FOR ANSWERS

- Everything really does boil down to **EDUCATION**. The more one learns the more one needs to learn. The more one knows the more one needs to know. The educated person knows his/her limitations; knows that no one has all the answers; knows facts are provable and that everything else is an opinion. Abstract, that which is not concrete, has different meanings for different people.

- The black community finds itself in dire straits because it is a **fragmented community** with shallow modern roots due to a history of poverty and isolation. Blacks have only enjoyed the right of the majority for a little over half a century. They had the traditions, customs, and languages of Africa, but those were eradicated. The black person is truly Americanized with the concept of excessive consumerism as well as a belief in the American dream. The latter a dying fantasy. The dream never existed for all.

- Detroit offered that dream with factory jobs which no longer exist. Hollywood offered it when Motown got into making movies. These movies produced stereotypes of the angry aggressive black male and the hypersexual, arms-akimbo, controlling female. As Malcolm X said: "You've been hoodwinked . . . led astray, bamboozled . . . sold a bill of goods." A broken shallow culture cannot build its foundation on the brawn and physical appearance of a small group of super men. Martin Luther King, Jr. referred to the "American Negro" as though as a separate species. As people without standing in society due to their inferior status, they can evolve by gaining education, housing, and employment not by chasing material wealth.

A PHILOSOPHY OF LIFE:

- I often ask people who seek advice from me, "What is the reason behind living?" They generally can't answer. They have never thought about it. Consequently, they continue their programmed day to day lives on automatic struggle. Many have no clue. When asked, and rarely, I tell them that life is very simple: you are born; you reproduce; you die. Minimally, life is reproducing and continuing the species. Most people simply reproduce the tribe. With the integration of tribes, comes the miscegenation of the races. Yes, your children are going to marry outside the tribe. Black women can't find suitable black men because men are less fixated on ethnicity or because black men are being incarcerated at a higher rate than other men.

- Again, religion and belief systems make life more meaningful. I tell others that I don't criticize religion. I criticize what people do with religion for their own gain. In fact, people would be more brutal without a god looking over their shoulders—higher powers are needed to ensure minimal civility. Religion, on the other hand, has always been contradictory—I am a man of logic and science.

- People without a purpose for living, a purpose not based in more than material gain, will always need something: a bigger house, a nicer car, another million dollars in the bank, more children, thinner bodies, nicer clothes etc. Such is human nature. There are millions of discoverers and free thinkers in jobs that are not suited for them. Men of profit and gain become men of philanthropy when they have to be. Men of honor and glory have to be in the ARENA. If everything has to be concrete and tangible for you to understand (males), your life tends to be shorter. Nature favors the evolver—the one who is empathetic and magnanimous. Men who retire without anything else to do generally perish. They generally defined themselves by on automatic perfunctorily mundane behaviors and practices.

JUST WHO DO I THINK I AM

Professionally, I can speak to the material presented here both because of my training and my career. My formal training has resulted in degrees and certifications in foreign language, education and Psychological Services. I am a professional teacher, but I have also worked as a custodian's assistant and for the U.S. Post Office. As a teacher, I have worked in different areas of the country with young people and adults. I have taught children with special needs and adults in both basic education and institutional settings.

Personally, I have lived in many parts of the country. I grew up poor but have entered the middle class. I have been bullied by those who thought themselves better than me. I have suffered from racial discrimination and benefited from affirmative action. I flirted with substance abuse and turned from it. I also face mental health issues and have taught myself to deal with those issues and function successfully. I am iconoclastic, reclusive, and dismissive. This view allows me to objectively examine many aspects of group human behavior that appear hard to comprehend.

What follows is an autobiography that will detail my experiences and education.

I was born in 1950 in Rutherford County Tennessee (Murfreesboro), 32 miles southeast of Nashville. I am one of seven children, four boys and three girls. My parents were Annie Elizabeth, "Momma", and her husband, Henry Thomas, "Henry." Henry's father was known as "Daddy." Apparently Momma and Henry made a pact in which he would claim all of us as his legitimate children. At 12, a schoolmate informed me that Henry Thomas was not my father. His brother, my father's age, told him that I was a bastard, that Henry had been cuckolded. Years later, the two children that Henry acknowledged as his true issue were listed as his heirs. Daddy had been seriously injured and rendered blind after an explosion somewhere near Smyrna, Tenn. After the explosion, Daddy acquired some property. Henry inherited that property and subsequently left it only to the two children he accepted as his own.

My childhood was one of poverty. We never had less than 12 people living in the small house that "Daddy" built with his own hands. We did have electric lights but could not use them if it was raining for fear of being electrocuted. Water came from a tap in the yard and a limited amount of heat came from a single stove. Ours was a worse living condition than that of many but outhouses were common in my world. Only those with jobs at the college (Middle Tennessee State) or other businesses that hired "Coloreds" or "Negroes" had indoor plumbing.

My three brothers and I slept in a small crawl space of an attic. Momma and Henry, when he was there, slept in the area next ours. We were hungry most of the time and lived off a diet of pinto beans and wildlife killed during the hunting season, mostly rabbits and fish. In the summer, we had a garden that produced green beans, field peas, corn, okra, and tomatoes. The whites on the edge of town had fields of turnips, and they allowed the "colors" to gather the top. In the fall, we picked cotton at $.03 a pound. The most I picked was 43 pounds, earning more than a dollar for working in the fields all day from the late sunrise of fall to the early sunset. The middle of the day was hot but more tolerable than the summer heat of the Mid South. Ma Vic, Victoria Pates, was Daddy's diabetic mother. She took me to the fields with her while dismissing the others as "lazy, good-for-nothings wenches."

Every Saturday night, Ma Vic would take me to the kitchen for company while she made biscuits and prepared the chicken for frying the next morning. As she worked, she talked about lots of things that I did not understand, but she reinforced that I was a good boy; that I had "muthatwit." I assume she credited me with a type of ageless wisdom—something like an old soul.

Ma Vic was not overly religious but made occasional supplication of the "LAWD" She could not attend church because she was hobbled by arthritis and diabetes. In fact, I witnessed her lose a finger to diabetes. I remember that she got $30 or 40 dollars a month in social security payments. Momma got $18 a week cleaning houses.

I grew up in the segregated South and thus was surrounded by the values of the time. I suffered from an inferiority complex as a result of constant rejections due to undesirable physical traits. I had always been called a skinny, ugly kid with nappy, bad hair. I was born with a high sensitivity to rejection and the childhood cruelty that children show to one another

I was miserable in school. Kids are cruel and I imagine I was just as cruel to others as they were to me; but children, without options, choose to become the victim. My memories of the teachers are not pleasant one. They looked down upon us provincials and laughed behind our backs at our lack of sophistication. Once a teacher dropped me off at home and insisted on coming in. She was shocked at the abject poverty that she found: a big stove in the middle of the floor provided the only heat;

the floor was made of boards of wood covered with dirt. This teacher, like the all the teachers at the school, was newly graduated from the teachers college at Tennessee A and I, now Tennessee State. She seemed fascinated by the poverty and asked questions about the house: Who cleaned? Why was the house so dirty? What did we eat? Did we have a bathroom? How many people lived there?

These teachers made fun of the provincials, their students, in Murfreesboro, Tenn. They spent the school year in the country and returned to Nashville and other cities during the summer. We had new ones every year. From this experience, I cultivated a dislike for the Negro bourgeoisie or 'bourgie Negroes' in the vernacular. I would later label them the petty bourgeois upon reading college level sociology. Poor black children have to deal with these attitudes even today from middle class teachers. Young males from poor environments can sense that judgmental rejection from teachers who are more concerned with nails, hair, and dress.

In what I assume was an effort to *encourage* good hygiene, my 3rd grade teacher went around the room pointing out who had on clean clothes and who did not. She skipped identifying me as one who came to school in clean clothes. I asked her to reconsider. She admitted that I had clean clothes most of the time. Momma taught us how to wash and iron early. I was determined to have clean clothes.

In the 5th grade, I had an experience that has left me emotionally scarred. The teacher led the class in bullying me verbally. One by one they took turns telling me what a miserable creature I was. One girl said that she would kill herself, if she had to marry me. The teacher joined in, and I just put my head down on the desk and cried as the bullying continued for what seemed like forever . . .

Academically I was always among the top 3 in the class. Consequently I managed to avoid the beatings that the teachers gave students who did not have memories for rote learning. But, I trembled at the thought of physical education. Because I lacked the physical prowess required, I was subject to more nasty, bullying remarks. On Sunday nights, I cried over the fact that I would have to go to school the next day. At that point in my life, I decided to get even by living well—by educating myself so that I would never have to ask anyone for anything. I had few friends and lived in a fantasy world of imaginary friends. I was not good at sports, so I wasn't accepted by my male peers, nor was I interested in the mischief that they were getting into. My mother Elizabeth and Great Grandmother Victoria were my only supporters at the house. Regardless of what I have or may yet accomplish, I still harbor a sense of inadequacy and cope with psychological misgivings and doubts stemming directly from the hurt inflicted at that period in my life.

When I was 12 years old, I talked Momma into piano lessons from Reverend Francis for $0.50 a lesson and threw myself obsessively into banging on the old upright piano (missing most of the keys) in the front room. My siblings sorely resented that she was willing to do this for me. My brothers and sisters as well as most of the grown folks around me compounded my sense of alienation. I knew I had to get out of that environment, or I be handicapped for life by it.

Lucky for me, my mother's mother, Bertha Watkins, known to me as Ma Bertha, agreed to let me come to live with her in Detroit. Henry Thomas flatly refused to send me. But Uncle "Meat," Henry's university educated brother, got me an $8 dollar Greyhound Bus ticket to Michigan in August of 1964. Henry said that I could stay for the summer, but I had no intentions of returning. When Henry Thomas learned of my plans to stay, he threatened to have me taken away to reform school. I spoke up to him for the first time, I told him that he had done nothing for me, that Uncle Meat had bought us clothes which he, Henry, wrote off on his taxes; that I would go to reform school before I would return to Tennessee. He relented.

Struggling as I was to get from day to day while living in Tennessee, I was oblivious to the civil rights movement. But, the world opened up for me in Detroit. There were educational opportunities and middle class black people of position and power on Detroit's northwest side. I was an average student but made an impression on the white teachers who identified me as having potential.

We lived on the corner of Northlawn Street and Pembroke Avenue, a lower middle class neighborhood of mostly black factory workers and other blue collar workers in Northwest Detroit, 3 blocks from 8 Mile Rd, the street that separated the blacks from whites. Most of the people in my new neighborhood could trace their roots to the Southern States, especially AL, GA, TN, and MS.

I was to attend MacDowell Middle School. My college educated uncle told me that, on the first day of school, I was to insist that I be put in the college prep curriculum. I was not placed in that program, however. Instead, I was tracked into the blue collar course study which included typing, bookkeeping, regular math, and English. I remember all blacks in the class and one white girl. The whites were tracked higher.

I also remember that those black classes in which I was placed were rowdy and chaotic. We had a class called 'auditorium'. I don't even remember what we did in there, possibly performing arts. I remember the white auditorium teacher saying." Go ahead and finish killing me with your behavior. I have already had a breakdown."

I had never had white teachers for I had gone to segregated schools in Rutherford County, Tennessee. What black parents and their children didn't realize was that these were liberal Northern whites, second generation immigrants. The tribal nature of groups made it difficult for Southern blacks to distinguish friend from foe. All whites were racists; all whites were the same.

The junior high students were cruel to me for being from the south. Bullying was the nature of the junior high schoolers (middle school now). Consequently, I kept my mouth shut because they laughed at my accent and my clothes. But I earned good grades. The white and Jewish teachers would grab and hug me. They all knew of me as the smart, quiet one.

While much better than in Tennessee, the situation in my new home was not good. My grandmother was living with a man, Warjack, from Georgia who had three daughters and a son. Warjack's daughters were resentful of my arrival. I slept on the floor or the couch.

My existence was like that of the immigrant Caribbean or African child. I was not allowed to associate with the neighborhood children. My grandmother, Bertha, told me that I was better than they; that I had a future; that they would only get me in trouble. Few students in the lower tracked classes applied themselves. I did not need to study to make good grades. I have an above average capacity for rote learning-memorization. Since I was not allowed to be on the streets at night, I had to look for other things to occupy me. I began listening to a 50K watt station well into the night and reading "strange" literature about German philosophers. I also became obsessive about learning the Spanish I heard on a station transmitting from New Orleans: LA VOZ DE RADIO CUBA LIBRE (the voice of free Cuba.

I wanted to know what they were saying, so I went to the library almost daily to check out Spanish books. I read the books from cover to cover becoming frustrated at not finding the conjugation of verbs. In the text you might find a past tense of an irregular verb. Ex: hice (I made, did) which comes from the infinitive hacer meaning to do or to make. Hice is not found in the dictionary. You have to know from where all these conjugated forms come. I had to check out a book of 201 Spanish conjugated verbs from the library to accomplish what I wanted.

We were struggling to remain in the neighborhood in a substandard house that the neighbors wanted condemned. At the time, I didn't understand why they were trying to protect their property values. I had come from the South (Murfreesboro, TN) where pigs were kept within the city limits, and no one ever received a code violation. In the segregated South all blacks lived within blocks of each other. Professionals, school teachers, and those with jobs at the college (Middle Tennessee State) complained about our livestock in the city, but did little officially to stop it. However, in Detroit, with more middle class incomes came concern for maintaining property values.

We cut our grass. Then, lower middle class "cut the grass"—no grooming and landscaping lawns. Waste water on grass?—No way! My grandmother even put out some mums that would last until the first snow. Consequently, I learned about perennials and annuals. At the same time, we had a small garden in the backyard where we grew tomatoes, greens, beans, onions and peppers. I was annoyed having to water and weed but as an adult I was fortunate to have learned how to garden. The neighbors would imitate and experiment with flowers pots on the porch and around the trees.

In spite of the fact that my grandmother set the standard in care for her yard, we were forced to move for several reasons. The house was substandard; it did not have a basement. My grandmother was told that all houses in Detroit had to have a basement. Also, a church wanted the lot for a parking lot. Beyond that we did not "fit in". Our car was more than 20 years old in a city where people got cars every 2 or 3 years. And, we were rubes fresh from the South without class or sophistication our car was more than 20 years old in a city where people got cars every 2 or 3 years. Foremost, we had to leave because we reminded the neighbors of poverty that they had managed to escape in the South

In 1966, the house was condemned, and we were forced to move to Richton and 12th Street (Rosa Parks Blvd). This was the ghetto, around the corner from where the Detroit riots started. My grandmother informed me that I could not attend Central High School. She knew I would not make it at Central High. Even then, the bullies and thugs ran the school. Instead of Central, I would take 3 buses to Mumford on the Northwest side. The winter ride was brutal: fierce winter winds that cut through you.

Ma Bertha worked as a domestic for a Jewish psychiatrist, Dr. Dorman, and brought Jewish food and culture home with her. I read the books that the Dormans gave to my grandmother. Mrs. Dorman also sent art into my world. In order to make room for new acquisitions, Mrs. Dorman sent the discarded pieces of art home with Ma Bertha. Although she only had an 8th grade education and learning disabilities, Ma Bertha's exposure to educated Jews all her life made her aware of the importance of an education. I

In Detroit, I asked for a social worker because I was being emotional abused by my grandmother (undiagnosed bipolar). The initial contact I had with a social worker was with a kindly empathetic gray haired white lady. I had never experienced such genuine concern. I told her of the verbal abuse and was introduced to the black department head of the Social Services Department for the school district. She obtained employment for me as a custodial assistant at a Detroit elementary school and a second job at the main post office in Detroit. I was amazed at how she could pick up the phone, explain my situation to her friends and get me a job.

At 16 years old, with the 2 jobs, I ran away and lived in a rooming house. I went back home after a few months and all was forgiven since I was paying room and board. I had never been out at night until I ran away. I now realize that avoiding the streets of Detroit as a teen saved me.

By the 10th grade, I was able to read Spanish. After 4 years of high school Spanish at Mumford High, my mastery of Spanish was a key to my getting into the University of Michigan. My years at Michigan were enlightening, but here again I was out of place with the children of upper middle class whites and blacks.

I never drank until my freshman year at college. My grandmother did not allow alcohol or cards in the house. At the time, an 18 year old could legally drink in Michigan. One night I drank so much beer that I verged on alcohol poisoning. I was sick all night and the next day. My affluent upper class classmates bought beer kegs and bags of weed.

I self-medicated with the drug de jour on campus: LSD, mescaline, amphetamines, black beauties (a diet pills) easily obtained with forged prescriptions, cocaine but not heroin. It was rumored two dudes on the second floor of the dorm could get anything. Such experimentation was common place. Presidents Kennedy, George Bush, Clinton, and Obama all admit to experimentation. My great aunt and her husband drank beer from dawn to dusk but never felt they were alcoholics because heavy beer drinkers are not considered alcoholics in the black community. I flirted with alcoholism for a few years, but rejected it after I was educated to the consequences. All the males in my family had been alcoholics or heavy drinkers.

Luckily for me, I did not have the brain chemistry of the other males in my family and was able to stop drinking. However, I do have an addictive/obsessive personality which manifests in a continual quest for achievement: a defense mechanism to counter the inferiority complex common to youths from abject poverty.

While in college, I learned that my mother was dying of cancer. She left Henry Thomas and moved to Detroit where she got medical help at Woman's Hospital, Detroit. She died a short time afterward. I dropped out of school when my mother died, and the University of Michigan sent my name, as required, to the draft board. I told the draft board that I would not go. No prosecution ensued since they found a heart murmur and disqualified me for service. I returned to the university earning a BA degree in Spanish in August1972 and receiving my teaching certificate in December. Murray-Wright High School in Detroit hired me as a Spanish Teacher.

In Detroit, it was strikes and threats of strikes in the70's and 80's and a superintendent, Arthur Jefferson, who was always involved in one crisis after another. I was hired fresh from college to teach high school Spanish at an inner city high school. I remained there from 1973 to 1981. I left because I was told that I would never be able to transfer out. The only black Spanish teacher at Mumford High School, Laura Prillerman, had become department chair at Ford High School on the Northwest side, and she wanted me to join her staff. Bob Boyce, the principal, told me that I should be happy where I was; that I had perfect class sizes; that when he got another black male Spanish teacher he would let me go. I taught there for 9 years before leaving for Oakland, California

I was diagnosed with Anxiety Disorder in the early 70's after the death of my mother and my entrance into the teaching profession in inner city Detroit. I had come from the controlled environment of the University of Michigan social sciences, education, and languages departments. I found the transition to the real world to be brutal as I faced institutional politics and students with special needs on all levels. I suffered from panic attacks and sleep disorders that almost disabled me. The doctor prescribed Librium and later Valium to cope with the chaos of a school system labeled a "MORASS" by a downriver (S.E. MICHIGAN) judge in the late 70's. I took the medication for 10 years.

The side effects of the Librium and Valium became worse and worse. I was drowsy and depressive all the time. In addition, I was numbed and zombie-like. I had grown to take on an existentialistic view of life. There was no great zest to live: *Life is a bitch, and then you die* became my mantra.

Even in the face of this depressed state, I remained an avid reader. I read both the Detroit News and Free Press from cover to cover daily. I also subscribed to 4 or 5 magazines from Times and Newsweek to Science, Entertainment and Professional magazines. I read about Seasonal Affective Disorder (SAD) in the late 70's.and concluded that

I had most of the symptoms: lack of energy in the months of limited sunshine. In Michigan those months are December, January, February. Michigan has more cloudy days than most states. I also had a great appetite for sweets and a debilitating depression that lasted all winter long. I would pray for shorter winters. I lived for the increasing daylight of February. I was particularly aware that in the years that winter ended in March, as it should, I experienced an immediate mood change. I acquired a sun lamp and exercised inside. In 1977, I began a regimen of exercise and diet that continues to this day. I jog 3 or 4 times a week with alternating days of strength building exercises. My family cannot accept my health regime. They tell me "to get some meat on my bones" at 5'7" I am 155lbs, 32" waist—my consistent size,

I moved to the Hollywood Hills, CA in the fall of 1982. My mood changed immediately. I was able to jog or walk daily. Exposure to the sun after running would increase the runner's high produced by endorphins and more oxygen to all parts of the body. How much of Detroit's populace, especially those from the Sun Belt, suffer as I did? How many are aware of such a disorder? How many self-medicate? I would never be able to live above a certain latitude again unless I was able to have extensive lighting and jogging and walking paths with natural fauna and flora. There must be a connection with nature in all seasons.

Ten years later, I was diagnosed with bipolar disorder by Kaiser Permanente Mental Health in Cobb Co, Georgia. The doctor prescribed Lithium (It was cheap.), Prozac, and Depakote. I could not tolerate Lithium but used the Prozac and Depakote until I lost insurance coverage in 2001. I have been without insurance coverage since then. Due to my medical history, without the Affordable Care Act, I would never be able to get medical coverage. I can afford to see a Physician

Assistant. My blood pressure is normal to borderline 120-140/80-90, and my cholesterol level is under 200. I exercise 6-7 times a week, rain or shine, heat or cold to control my disorders without the pharmaceuticals. But most important, I limit my exposure to stress and stress givers. By contrast, I hear that my siblings have all the ethnically based medical problems.

Using The Diagnostic and Statistical Manual of Disorders, I have self-diagnosed myself with ADHD and Obsessive—Compulsive Disorder based in the dysfunctional nature of my childhood and/or body chemistry. I am unable to concentrate for long periods of time, thus it is hard for me to complete tasks. I started piano lessons and lost interest. I have attempted to author more than 12 books. This is the first to be completed. My handwriting is characteristically that of a person with ADHD: great variety of lettering with caps and small letters used inconsistently, impulsive/interrupting behavior. In classes, I never raised my hand; I just blurted things out. In addition, I am inattentive and hyperactive. I cannot be still for a long period of time. Many people consider me rude or arrogant because I pass notes during meetings and avoid social situations. I am impatient because a few minutes can seem like an hour. Most drivers on the road get in my way, and I am dismissive of people who are more deliberate in their movements.

In reflecting upon my obsessive—compulsive behaviors, I recognize my inability to know when/if they reach a debilitating level. Since this disorder is self-diagnosed, it may or may not be an accurate assessment. But I can recognize qualities from my past that support my self-diagnosis. As a teen, I sat and practiced the piano for hours and hours then I lost interest. In learning foreign languages, I got books from the library and used a dictionary to look up every word in the book. I became very frustrated as I was trying to learn Romance Languages which have millions of conjugated verb forms in 15 tenses or more. The language dictionary gave me only infinitive verb forms not the conjugated verb forms I require.

I do not have many ritual types of behaviors such as excessive hand washing; however, I do check the iron and stove often. I obsess over matters of my personal financial and physical security. I compulsively pick up the litter in the block alongside my house. I am able to function but some individuals need treatment if their practices interfere with daily functioning.

In Oakland, I started as an ESL teacher and rose quickly to be a Teacher On Special Assignment who trained teachers in language acquisition methodologies to immigrant children. While working in the district bilingual office in Oakland, I was offered a leadership position at Calvin Simmons Junior High without being credentialed in school leadership. I was working as a TSA (teacher on special assignment) in the bilingual office of the school district. My charge was to review bilingual and E S L programs for state and federal compliance. I had contacts in more than 20 Oakland schools. When I arrived, the black project directors (administrative assistants) were relieved that I was black. Subsequently, I was offered positions for which I was not qualified. One administrative official told me that I could work on credentialing later.

My degree in Spanish (University of Michigan) and bilingual certification (Wayne State University, Detroit) had caught the attention of a white personnel director who wanted to improve the quality of education in the district. I was first hired as a Spanish teacher at Oakland Tech; and, by the next year, I had a title at Roosevelt Junior

High-School as Director of ESL. I replaced a white male who was more qualified than I. My quick rise earned the dislike of most staff members many of whom had been waiting for promotions.

In 1986 I was languishing—living in two rooms in an expensive hilltop home in Oakland-Berkeley Hills. I was working in the bilingual office of the Oakland Unified School District. ALL the politics of the district were stressing me. In Oakland, I encountered the same racial politics shared by all big city systems: race, immigrant population, gender, shrinking tax base, teacher salaries and strikes, affluent vs. poor and transient communities, superintendent and school board issues.

The state of California had mandated that the school system address the needs of immigrant children. But, the black community was indifferent to or outright hostile to the immigrant communities. When I told one of my administrators that the black kids were bullying the Asian and Latino kids, he informed me that they needed to know abuse and discrimination. I worked in Oakland from 1982 to 1986 then I walked away when I could no longer tolerate the abuses of the system.

In Oakland it was the cabal of black females and their minions who held power in the district. Some of these people have since been convicted of certain crimes and gone to jail (mid and late 80's and 90's). I never lasted long in any district because of my sense of being exploited by those at the top of the pyramid.

While still in Detroit, I had begun an MA in Bilingual Education at Wayne St University, an Historic Black University. Upon leaving California, I looked to a return to the South to attempt another master's degree at an HBCU—Atlanta University—The institution of black intellectuals such as W.E.B. Dubois. I arrived in Atlanta on New Year's

Eve 1986 and began studies on a degree in psychological services shortly afterward. Atlanta University is now Clark Atlanta University.

Two years later, having completed the degree, I came up against what I considered unethical practices of the school in the form of unreasonable graduation fees. I do not attend ceremonies and this graduation was no exception. The office staff had never heard of anyone not attending graduation. They insisted I would have to pay anyway. I told them to keep the degree, but I would need transcripts. Several years later I was able to get transcripts.

Soon after arriving in Atlanta, I started substitute teaching at a neighborhood school in Fulton County. The sub's job turned into a full time position in a few months for the Fulton County School District. I stayed with Fulton County for two years and then moved on. I continued my leap from job to job in education until I realized that I needed to look at retirement. The usual stint for a teacher is around 3-5 years.

Teaching is a difficult job with great rewards if you have the right support and funding. I always found myself in a morass of educational mediocrity: Detroit, Oakland, and in Georgia, South Fulton County, South Cobb County, and the ethnically and racially changing Marietta City. It has become obvious that public education will always be a battleground for politicians and educationalistas. Students and their teachers are the casualties.

Over the years, I have pursued my personal education. I have various degrees of fluencies in the Romance languages except Romanian. When time permits I am working on the Greek, Arabic, Russian, and Korean alphabets. So far, I find Chinese characters daunting. I am an avid reader on topics ranging from the origins of the universe to Zen enlightenment.

In traditional classrooms, I have taught Spanish, English, social studies, and even Latin and French for a short while. I currently teach adult ESL and GED. In less traditional settings, I have taught or am currently teaching in treatment programs and jails. Through it all, I have been searching for the place I belong, a place where the individual is respected and the effort to improve is supported.

I have always wanted to write, but one just does not go out and write just as one does not just go out and make a living as an artist or thespian. I have begun many writing projects only to put them down due to lack of access to publishers. In 2007, I made a call to inquire about self-publishing. One day in February of 2013, they returned my call asking me if I had been published as yet. It is time.

ABOUT THE BOOK

This is social commentary on issues that affect the black community. It is NOT a scientific study. These views are meant to stimulate exchanges about the pressing issues found in our culture: consumerism, relationships, values, public conduct, social strata, and matters of mental soundness, and the church etc.

The black community is reactive to comment on the church and the icons from the church. High ranking clergy are at the top of social hierarchy. I am not hostile to religion; I am expressing my opposition to what the Black church has become. In this matter, Some will be offended. Others, as is their nature, come to judge and reject, not to reflect on what is said. As Icona Oprah Winfred said, "You did not come to listen and learn, you came to judge" I anticipate an amen corner from those in the academic community who discuss these matters often.

My comments on non-standard speech of high profile individuals will be taken the wrong way, no doubt. My point is simple: When exhorting young people to educate themselves you have to be consistent. They will emulate that speech. It is hypocritical to address conditions that your actions perpetuate.

As a political junkie and avid reader, these are my unofficial gleanings borne of an oversaturation of exposure to all types of media and social outlets. Many of my views come from reactions to talk radio. A culture of talk radio types and personae have emerged on black talk radio, because you have the same people calling in daily with specious conspiracies.

The black community is not a single voice. We have great diversity of thought. Consequently, there will never be a consensus. I don't delude myself in believing that we will all be one big happy family. But we can do better.

www.ingramcontent.com/pod-product-compliance
Lightning Source LLC
Chambersburg PA
CBHW050410290526
45786CB00003B/1200